Scootin' Thunder

SCOOTIN' THUNDER

Beth Houser

iUniverse, Inc.
New York Lincoln Shanghai

Scootin' Thunder

Copyright © 2006 by Beth Houser

All rights reserved. No part of this book may be used or reproduced by any means, graphic, electronic, or mechanical, including photocopying, recording, taping or by any information storage retrieval system without the written permission of the publisher except in the case of brief quotations embodied in critical articles and reviews.

iUniverse books may be ordered through booksellers or by contacting:

iUniverse
2021 Pine Lake Road, Suite 100
Lincoln, NE 68512
www.iuniverse.com
1-800-Authors (1-800-288-4677)

ISBN-13: 978-0-595-40337-0 (pbk)
ISBN-13: 978-0-595-84713-6 (ebk)
ISBN-10: 0-595-40337-9 (pbk)
ISBN-10: 0-595-84713-7 (ebk)

Printed in the United States of America

To my father, Bob Houser, and the men of the 13th United States Army Air
Corps and B-24 crews who served in Guadalcanal,
Especially the crew of Scootin'Thunder.

Contents

PREFACE xi

PROLOGUE 1

Chapter 1 3

Chapter 2 9

Chapter 3 15

Chapter 4 21

Chapter 5 27

Chapter 6 35

Chapter 7 41

Chapter 8 45

Chapter 9 51

Chapter 10 55

Chapter 11 59

Chapter 12 65

Chapter 13 71

Chapter 14 105

Chapter 15 109

Chapter 16 115

Chapter 17 121

Chapter 18 129

Chapter 19 137

Chapter 20 147

Chapter 21 153

Chapter 22 157

Chapter 23 165

Chapter 24 171

Chapter 25 179

Chapter 26 187

Chapter 27 193

TRANSITION TO 2006 197

EPILOGUE 201

AFTERWORD 203

ACKNOWLEDGMENTS

I wish to thank first and foremost my father, Bob Houser, for finally caving in to my prodding and giving me his diaries he kept during the war. I have been asking him to write this story since I was a teenager and I guess I persisted just long enough and finally wore him down. I was ultimately able to convince him that others are interested and would enjoy reading about his adventures while stationed in Guadalcanal. I spent several hours with him asking questions and taking notes while he smoked his cigars.

Oscar Fitzhenry is a name I have heard as long as I can remember. When I contacted Oscar and told him I was going to write the story about Scootin' Thunder he immediately offered his help and assistance. Oscar supplied me with all the intelligence reports from all their missions along with the missing air crew reports and his personal diary. I finally got to meet Oscar and his wife, Ruth, along with Bill Harris in May 2005 while attending the 5th Bomb Group reunion in San Diego, California. I think Oscar was thrilled that I would be writing the story of his crew and Scootin' Thunder.

I would also like to thank Bill Harris and Joanne Emerick for supplying me with some additional pictures. Joanne is the historian for the 31st bomb squadron and editor of the Tail Winds newsletter. In addition, I would like to thank Jesse Unruh for the pictures of the Pretty Prairie Special crew stranded on the beach and of his father, Colonel Marion Unruh, when the P.O.W. camp was liberated in September 1945.

Thank you to Chris Berry who took time out from his job and school to edit the first draft of the manuscript. I appreciate all the comments and corrections. I am also very grateful to the extra editorial help I received from Joe Vranich; his comments and suggestions were invaluable and thought provoking. I would also like to thank the many friends and family that listened intently and encouraged me through-out this journey; Maggie Kite, Marie Meade, Margie Moeller and of course, my mother, Elsa Houser.

PREFACE

I never gave much thought to my service back in 1943; besides it was 63 years ago. It wasn't that I was not proud, only that we had all served. When I was 22, and a second lieutenant, all I thought about was wearing a sharp looking uniform of a pilot, flying and getting into the battle as soon as possible. Everything at the time was exciting and a new adventure. I and no one I knew thought we would be the unfortunate ones to crash or die. I was just beginning my life and although I witnessed death and dying I didn't think it would touch me.

The men I served with on Scootin' Thunder shared a similar belief. We were sent to the South Pacific and Guadalcanal to fight from the vantage point of a B-24. Our plane took on a special significance, primarily to us. Several squadrons with their planes and crews, each with ten men, felt the same, I am sure. We did what we had to do and hoped and prayed we would safely make it back to our airfield. The names and faces of my crew mates are forever etched in my mind. Familiar landmarks: Henderson, Carney, Koli, Ballale, Bougainville, Kahili, Rabaul, Munda, Kavieng, New Ireland; once clear, sharp images, are now faded with time and the murky memory of an 85-year-old.

I was one of the lucky ones and made it home to restart my life. This time it included my wife and seven children. I hardly ever spoke of Guadalcanal. When I did, it was relaying a couple of stories that stood out among all the rest. I spoke of Fitzhenry's skill as a pilot, Garman's pride and uncanny ability to navigate us to safety every time, and Harris' wild escapades. I got on with my life and looked ahead to my responsibilities as a husband and father. The South Pacific and 1943 waned and dimmed to near oblivion.

In 2003, after open heart surgery, I was in rehab at Long Beach Memorial Medical Center with six other men. The nurse put us through our bi-weekly workouts. At the end of our class the nurse called for a cool down period and congratulated all of us for completing with flying colors. One man commented, "The last time I worked out this hard I was in the Marines." Another man asked, "Where did you serve?" "Guadalcanal," he said. Surprised, the second man chirped, "I was in the Navy and I too was at Guadalcanal." I laughed and said, "Me too! I was with the Army Air Corps." The remaining four chimed in: "I was there too! So was I!"; another Air Corps guy, two Army and another Navy man. All of us had shared a similar experience overlapping times of a place called Guadalcanal. We sat around for a while and talked about places we had all seen from the eyes of young men. I listened and looked into the faces of all these old gentlemen and witnessed the spark of their faded youth, diminished by time. What did it mean? How and why we all were brought together at this time?

I left the group with a deeper appreciation and understanding of the time I spent back in 1943 and all the sacrifices so many had made. I reflected on those life-altering experiences and felt proud of these other men and myself for our contributions toward winning the war. Once young boys, now seasoned old men contemplating our service and the war that united us. I can finally say out loud, "I am proud to have served at Guadalcanal in the Army Air Corps with a great bunch of young guys on a B-24 Liberator named Scootin' Thunder.

G.R.Houser

PROLOGUE

A mother takes her reluctant 16-year-old son with her to an antique store. She needs him to help her put a small table in their car. She is busy talking to the owner while the boy wanders through the cluttered store.

The boy scans through some old books, passes by some old clocks and radios and looks up to see a bunch of framed pictures next to some old mirrors. A black and white 8x10 picture in an oak frame catches his eye. The picture shows two rows of servicemen standing in front of a large plane. The picture is from World War II. The boy stares intently at each face in the group. All ten men appear to be looking squarely back at the young boy. He looks at the plane and notices the name painted on the nose—"Scootin' Thunder"—with a lightning bolt piercing the moon.

The boy is mesmerized by the photo and can only hear the ticking of an old clock near him. The owner walks by the boy and notices his scrutiny of the picture. He asks the boy if he likes airplanes. The kid answers, "Yeah." The owner replies, "That plane there, son, is a B-24, called the Liberator." The kid says, "These guys must be Air Force." The owner responds, "In World War II they were called the Army Air Corps." The boy asks, "I wonder where this picture was taken?" The owner glances at the picture and then back at the boy "Can't say for sure. More B-24s were built than any other plane during World War II; they were used in Europe and in the Pacific theaters."

The boy looks as though he is trying to record each little detail of the picture to memory. He asks the owner, "Do you think any of these planes are still around? How old do you think these guys are?"

"What? In the picture?" the owner responds. "I bet they aren't much older than you. If you're asking about today, I would guess these young men would have to be in their 80s."

The kid asks, "How much do you want for this picture?" The older man looks at the picture and then back at the boy and says, "For you, since you're such a history buff, ten dollars."

The boy makes the purchase with small bills and assorted change and leaves the antique store with his mom. When they reach home, the boy takes the picture to his room looking for a suitable place to hang it. He places the picture on the bed and decides to remove it from the frame. He flips the picture over and sees, printed neatly on the back,

Guadalcanal 1943, Henderson Field
5th Bomb Group, 72nd Bomb Squadron.
1st Lt. Oscar Fitzhenry, Pilot
2nd Lt. G.R. Houser, Co-Pilot

The boy grabs a tablet from his desk and writes down all the information. He fits the picture back neatly into the frame and places it just above his desk. The boy sits at his desk and types into his computer: "Guadalcanal." A website takes him to some historical information.

It's late and the boy is getting ready for bed. Outside it is raining hard. He lies on his bed propped up by a pillow, listening to the rain. A flash of lightning and a crack of thunder are heard and the boy glances at the picture one last time before drifting off to sleep. The sound of the pounding rain is replaced by the droning sound of the B-24.

The next scene is the air base in Alamogordo, New Mexico, January 12, 1943.

Chapter 1

January 12, 1943 Tuesday
Airbase at Alamogordo, New Mexico

1st. Lt. Oscar Fitzhenry drove a jeep up to the PX on base and entered carrying a large brown envelope. Oscar is 5 feet 11 inches; mostly muscle compacted into his 157 pounds. His eyes are as dark as his black hair as he scanned the small group of soldiers milling about; he saw a few lieutenants standing near a counter became impatient and shouted out...

"Is there a Lt. G.R. Houser here? "GRRH, he mumbled to himself, what kind of a name is GRRH?" I stepped toward him and answered,

"I'm Lt. Houser."

"What does the G.R. stand for?"

"George Robert, I replied, but I go by Bob." I am the same height and weight as Oscar but with dark brown hair and eyes. I could tell immediately that Oscar was more outgoing than my more reserved self.

"Okay, Bob. I'm Oscar Fitzhenry and you can call me Fitz. Only my folks call me Oscar, and usually when they're angry with me." Oscar offered a wide smile and we shook hands. Fitz held up a brown envelope and said, "It looks like you're my co-pilot, according to these orders. I see you asked for an overseas assignment as soon as possible. Are you in some kind of hurry to get shot down?"

I chuckled, "No, not if I'm with a good pilot. Besides, I need a change of scenery."

Fitz laughed and said, "Where ya from, Bob?"

"Logansport, Indiana."

Fitz noticed stationery, envelopes, cigars and a journal that I was about to purchase. "You must be planning on writing a bunch of letters to your sweetheart back in Indiana," said Fitz.

"No, not anymore, it seems she's decided on some other guy." I said without emotion.

"Oh, so you're nursing a broken heart."

"Geez, I'm 22. I'm not ready to settle down."

"I get it," Fitz cracked, "She's ugly, right?"

"No, she's okay." I answered half-heartedly.

"Okay? What do you expect from Logansport? Hell, everyone knows the prettiest gals are from San Antonio."

"Really!" I said, "And where are you from?"

I finished my purchase and put a few cigars in my breast pocket.

Fitz looked at me in disbelief. "San Antonio, Texas, and they happen to have a lot of brave, handsome men as well."

"I thought I detected an accent…I wouldn't know about any 'brave or handsome' men. Didn't they all die at the Alamo?" I teased as I tossed my duffel bag into the back of the jeep, gingerly placing a heavy black box with a handle next to it.

"Yeah, I suppose. What's that?" asked Fitz.

"My Remington typewriter, I take it almost everywhere."

Fitz smiled "Well, I suppose if we run out of bombs, we could toss that heavy old thing at the Japs. Let's go get some lunch and I'll tell ya all you've been missing. I'm 21 and ya don't see me mooning over some gal from Logansport." We both laughed, and got into the jeep.

Fitz said, "We have orders to pick up the rest of the crew, then get our plane at Hamilton Field in San Francisco," as he adjusted his sunglasses. I smiled and said, "Sounds like a plan."

"I know where we can get some great Mexican food and see some pretty gals all at the same time," said Fitz. "What do you say, George Robert?"

"Make that Bob!"—The words lost under Fitz's Texas "yee haw" as we drove off in a cloud of dust.

January 22, 1943 Friday

Fitz and I entered the officers' barracks looking for our newly assigned bombardier. It's Friday night and the guys are getting dressed for a night on the town. Fitz walked in and asked, "Where you boys off to?"

One of the young men answered, "White Sands, they have some local band playing at the cantina and we thought we'd check it out. You wanna a come along?"

I answered, "Thanks, but we have dinner plans too. Any of you guys know a second lieutenant named Harris?"

One guy answered, "Yeah, Billy; he's in the shower. If he doesn't hurry up he's gonna miss his ride and wind up walking into town." As if on cue, a young kid in a towel walked in, drying his curly blonde hair. He's small at 5 feet 7 and about 130 pounds.

Fitz extended his hand and said, "Hey Harris, I'm Oscar Fitzhenry and this is my co-pilot, Bob Houser. So you're our bombardier replacement? You look barely old enough to shave," Fitz laughed.

"I'm 20. I may be small but I can get the job done, if you know what I mean." Billy giggled to himself, his blue eyes twinkling mischievously. I raised an eyebrow and said, "Bill, we're going into town to have dinner with Garman and his wife."

"Who's Garman?" he asked.

"He's our navigator and we'd like you to join us." Fitz said.

"No thanks guys, I've got a ride into town with these boys. I can meet him later." Harris responded.

Fitz stated matter-of-factly, "Bill, you're coming into town with us, you're going to meet Garman and then you can make arrangements with your friends. This is my crew and I want to get all the introductions done tonight. Understand?"

"Sure, OK" Harris said. "Give me 15 minutes and I'll be ready."

"Make it five," I said, "I'm hungry and the Garmans will be waiting for us."

As we entered the White Sands' restaurant, several army personnel were dining and dancing. Standing next to the piano player was a young couple. The woman was singing along to a ballad being played; the man was in uniform. He noticed Fitz and me and the kid with us and motioned for us to come over.

Fitz and I removed our hats as Garman introduced us. "This is my wife, Lolly." We shook hands. Harris, still wearing his hat, got a nudge from Fitz. Harris, oblivious to his faux pas, responded with an irritated "What?" Fitz took the hat off Harris and handed it to him.

Garman looked at Harris and shook hands saying, "I'm Bill Garman, the navigator."

"Hey, I'm Billy Harris; bombardier. How about that, two Bills? I guess people will be getting us confused a lot."

Garman answered, "I don't think so, Junior."

Harris looked at Garman's wife, smiled, and then said to Bill, "Wow, she's a keeper. Hey, Billy G, where y'all from?"

Garman forced a smile and said, "Oklahoma. I taught math at the university, and the name is Bill. What about you, Junior?"

"Oh, I'm from Texas" said Harris. "I haven't done a whole bunch but now I'm gonna be seeing the world from a B-24. Sounds like fun. Can you believe it?"

Garman answered dryly, "Yeah, I'm sure it will be lots of fun."

"Well, I've got to be going, I'm meeting some buddies of mine," said Harris.

"It's been a pleasure to meet you Billy" said Lolly. "Do take care of yourself."

"Yeah, sure…nice to meet you too. I'll see you guys later," said Harris.

"Hey Junior, be at the officers' meeting room at 0630," shouted Fitz.

"Sure thing, Fitz; I'll see you all tomorrow."

As Harris was leaving I leaned over to Lolly and said, "I heard you singing; you have a beautiful voice."

"Oh, thank you Bob. Do you sing too?"

"Yeah, some, I had the lead in our school operettas."

"How about a duet?" she said.

Bill Garman said, "I can't carry a tune in a paper sack; you two enjoy yourselves. Fitz and I will get us a table and some drinks."

"Do you know 'I'll See You Again'?" Lolly asked me and the pianist. We sealed our new friendship with a duet.

CHAPTER 2

March 16, 1943 Tuesday
Big Springs, Texas

The four of us officers are in our barracks discussing our orders to be at San Francisco's Hamilton Field on April 1st. I'm typing a letter to my younger brother. Garman is reading a book. Fitz is reviewing a folder of paperwork while Junior Harris paces back and forth, preoccupied with thoughts about naming our B-24.

"I think we should call her 'Plane Jane'—you know, P-L-A-N-E and paint her reclining back, you know, with her arms behind her head and her legs in the air." He giggled, "You know, she could have blonde hair and she's not wearing a stitch of clothing." He seemed to be getting excited just visualizing it.

Garman sarcastically replied, "That's original, Junior, a naked blonde girl on the side of a plane. Why didn't I think of that?" He went back to his book.

Fitz laughed, "Come on guys, we need something different from all the others. It should be something that will represent *our* crew, something, I don't know, different and unusual. What do you think, Bob?"

I stopped typing, picked up a tablet and said, "I've been thinking about this for a while and wanted to see what you guys think. I've thought of a name that is unique and will definitely stand out from all the others."

Fitz said, "What is it?"

"Scootin' Thunder," I said. "I had drawn a rough sketch. It's a lightning bolt piercing the moon between the names, Scootin' and Thunder." Garman left his cot to take a look. "Let me see," he said.

I continued, "We'll be flying a heavy bomber and we'll strike like lightning, not like a P-38, but it's going to sound like thunder when the bombs drop and then we'll scoot on out of there! Therefore; Scootin' Thunder."

Fitz and Garman both smiled. Garman said, "I like it, yeah, Scootin' Thunder." Junior interrupted with, "What about a naked girl?"

Garman said, "Junior, if you want a naked girl go look for one, it's not going on our plane!" Fitz and I laughed. I went back to my letter, pounding away on the keys of my old Remington. Fitz continued staring at the sketch and seemed to need a bit more convincing as he said—slowly and deliberately—"Scootin' Thunder."

April 1, 1943 Thursday
Hamilton Field, San Francisco, Ca.

Our complete crew of 10 boarded the plane and stowed their gear getting ready for takeoff. The tail number painted on our B-24 read: 4240100. The nose art of

Scootin' Thunder with the lightning bolt piercing the moon had been painted on both sides of the plane.

Fitz yelled, "Clear!" and we heard Don Gorsuch's echoing "clear" as Fitz started engine number three. There was the cough then the pop-pop of the engine as it turned over and came to life spewing white smoke. He repeated the same procedure with engines four, then two, then one. The plane was revving with all her engines in sync as Fitz and I went through our list checking all the instruments in the cockpit.

Fitz said, "Gorsuch, how's the idle and fuel situation?" Crew chief Donaldson Gorsuch responded, "Fuel supply, is all, mixture is full rich, 2700 rpm; you're good to go, Lieutenant."

"Hawaii, here we come," said Fitz. The engines were droning on when Fitz turned to me with a huge grin and said, "Bob, what do ya say we scoot on out of here?" I noted the time, put my notebook into my breast pocket, next to a cigar, and said, "Let's do it!"

The lumbering B-24, with our newly formed crew, picked up speed racing down the runway and lifted into the beautiful clear blue sky for a perfect takeoff, destination Hawaii.

May 7, 1943 Friday
Hickham Field
Oahu, Honolulu

After several weeks in Hawaii, we got orders to leave Hickham airfield and head for Canton Island in the Phoenix Group. The trip to Guadalcanal in May and June 1943 was like a traveler's exotic itinerary with some distinctions.

First, Hickham Field at Honolulu, then off to Canton—a postage-stamp island with a coral runway sporting a single tree for decoration. The sight of a B-24 approaching this desolate outpost must have had the impact of a screeching pterodactyl to the abandoned souls at this forlorn spot. There for just one day, we moved on to the Fiji Islands, landing on Nandi in heavy rain. At 1900 we took off again for Noumea, New Caledonia, in very rough weather Garman, navigating, got us there right on the button.

While there I shopped for a pillow for my cot but didn't know how to ask our French-speaking clerks for it. It was no help for Fitz, the Texan, to try to establish rapport by trying his only exposure to extra-lingual conversation: "Esta Buena!"

No nets needed for sleeping quarters—the natives said the Nioli trees eliminated mosquitoes. We spent the next four days in New Caledonia before taking off for Espiritu Santo, a.k.a. Buttons, arriving May 14, 1943.

Our temporary lodgings at Buttons resembled a tent city. The tents had wood planking for the floors with cots accommodating four men per tent. The tents were hot and stuffy and in constant need of ventilation which proved to be a welcome sight for the local insect population. On several occasions we would encounter various rodents scampering through our makeshift home looking for a mislaid snack. The tents were randomly placed and at night some of the occupants from distant tents were silhouetted by a dimly lit lantern. Espiritu Santo was the staging area for squadrons about to be sent to Guadalcanal.

On May 20th we had an 11-hour search and patrol mission before returning to Buttons. We sighted on a convoy of three DDs American destroyers in our triangular hop. During our down time the boys looked for ways to pass the day including horseshoes, ping-pong and softball. Fitz managed to find a vagrant horse roaming the area and proceeded to ride him until he was thrown and suffered a severe sprained ankle in the spill. He named the horse Thumper but Fitz was the one that got thumped on his initial ride.

June 5, 1943 Saturday

Lieutenant Michael Lord, on a night takeoff from Buttons, ran into a wayward cow on the runway. The cow was killed, the plane badly damaged and the mission cancelled. Mike suffered unending teasing. However, the cow was butchered and the crews got a steak dinner out of the mishap. When Mike returned to his tent, nineteen year old navigator Lieutenant Melvin Tiemann, a.k.a. Timo, the original gremlin, walked past Mike and started the chain of wisecracks:

"Gosh Mike, what did that cow ever do to you?" Some of the guys made mooing sounds and another officer asked:

"Where did the plane get it? In the cowl flaps?"

"Did you see that crash?" "Yeah, it was udderly disgraceful."

Everyone in the tent laughed at Mike's expense as another guy shouted, "Well, the Lord giveth and the Lord taketh away isn't that right, Lieutenant?"

"Yeah, he giveth us all a steak dinner tonight!"

June 15, 1943 Tuesday

First Lieutenant Don Hathaway came into our tent shouting, "Hey guys, I just heard we're leaving for Guadalcanal in the morning."

Amid cheers, one of the first pilots Lieutenant John Epple said, "Finally, we get to see some action. I'm getting tired of throwing horseshoes."

Fitz, Epple and Hathaway were cadet classmates back in Texas all are first pilots and very close friends.

"It's about time" said Fitz—"This is great news. I guess we should start packing." Garman, after a quick look at his charts, said, "That's 557 miles from here. What time are we leaving?" "0600" said Hathaway. "It's going to be an early evening, fellas."

As I made a note in my diary, Fitz seemed truly excited. "This is it!" he said. "We're finally going to get some combat time." The excitement was catching—everyone scrambling about packing duffel bags and talking bravely about what they are going to do in combat.

Fitz aimed one at me: "You said you wanted a change of scenery, Houser, this is it. Write that in your diary."

"Yeah, that's why we all came to this party." I said.

Chapter 3

June 16, 1943 Wednesday
Arriving on Guadalcanal

We were up at 0400, packed and ready to go. Breakfast in the mess tent then we all piled into trucks that took us to the airfield. We were part of the 5th Heavy Bomb Group. Our squadron, the 72nd, consists of 12 B-24s. It was 0635 and our turn to take off for Guadalcanal. The guys were eager and jumped on the plane like fleas leaving a dog. Scootin' Thunder, primed and ready to go, took off without incident.

We landed at 1030 on Guadalcanal, a.k.a. Cactus, at Henderson Field. We heard the field had been named for a Marine pilot that died at Midway. This island was about 90 miles long and 25 miles wide. The sky was clear with a slight breeze. The crew began removing their gear from the plane to waiting trucks for the ride to the barracks. Everyone was all smiles to finally be on this famous island when a war sound broke the congenial mood. We looked up to see just above us a fighter plane roaring across the sky—a P-39 chasing a Jap Zero. Surreal to us so-recently civilized—a dogfight at 12,000 feet. At first we were glued in our tracks. The staccato machine gun fire snapped us back to reality. Tracer bullets exploded on the ground 15 feet from us. It was a community belly flop into a nearby ditch. The Zero was hit and exploded in an orange and black burst. The P-39 continued streaking across the sky while the broken Zero wings fluttered down like a leaf, crashing into the sea.

Peeking from the ditch, we saw two P-38s, a P-39 and several Corsairs hot after three Zeros. All of the enemy planes were blasted out of the sky. The Jap planes were smoking and on fire as they all crashed into the sea.

We had no idea, until much later, that we had happened to land on Guadalcanal at the exact time that a major air attack was taking place over Tulagi, an island northeast of us. Later we were informed that this was the largest single day Allied air victory in the war with 79 Zeros being shot down and 17 more knocked out by ack-ack. Only six of our planes were lost. Welcome to the war, boys.

We gathered our gear and tossed it onto the trucks. All of us were eager after witnessing the P-39 attack that lone Zero. We knew then we were here to help "pin these boys' ears back."

It took us about 20 minutes to get from the airfield to our barracks. I walked into the officers' Quonset hut and selected a bed closest to the door. I placed my typewriter on my cot while I stowed my gear. Fitz took the bunk next to mine with Garman just on the other side of me. Junior was across the aisle rapidly tossing his things into the small closet between the bunks. The metal huts on Cactus were a welcome change from the suffocating tents on Buttons. Our hut was right next to the rivers edge and could house 10–15 men. The other huts were indiscriminately placed around the camp grounds with no particular order in their arrangement. It appeared to be a haphazard display yet proved to be a sound decision once the rains turned the hard ground into muddy sink holes. I soon discovered the fierce sound of the rain beating down on the roof resonated throughout the hut creating a tranquil environment.

"I want to take a look around and see what's on this island," said Junior.

"Don't go wandering off, Junior, we have a briefing at 1500, so you might want to get some lunch and settle in before checking out this place," said Fitz.

I mentioned to Garman that I was about out of cigars and wondered if they had any tobacco on this base. Junior volunteered, "I'll check it out and let you know." All of us went to the mess tent to get lunch.

At 1500 all the eager young crews were at the scheduled briefing awaiting their instructions. When were we going to see some combat? It was sooner than we thought.

We were told we would be taking off at 1730 for our first combat mission. The target raid was on Ballale. Our squadron was to target the runway at the southern end of Bougainville Island.

It was time to leave. All of the guys from our squadron got on the trucks that would take us to the airfield. It was a 20 minute ride over some rough roads. I looked up at a large sign that was strung up between two trees for all the crews to see. It read:

Kill the Bastards!
Down this road marched one of the Regiments of
The United States Army
Knights serving the Queen
Of Battles
Twenty of their wounded in litters were
Bayoneted, shot and clubbed
By the Yellow Bellies
Kill the Bastards!

Scootin' Thunder was waiting in the revetment just off the main runway loaded with 40 cluster frag bombs, full of fuel and ready for action. I only hoped we were as well.

We were in the first element of planes to take off. Several of the ships in the squadron experienced various mechanical problems and only eight of the B-24s were able to take off. We climbed to an altitude of 16,000 feet and flew in formation, reaching our target at 2022. The airfield of Ballale was clear and we unloaded 35 of our bombs on the side of the runway. The 5 remaining bombs failed to release from the racks of the bomb bay and we were forced to return and land with live bombs on board.

I got to thinking…A matter of days before we landed on Guadalcanal, Mark Rifkin, a co-pilot, and I had been watching the movie "Air Force" in a Honolulu theater. Now, today, two or three years beyond our teens, we had become the real-life characters of that movie. No more a theater seat, but cockpit and battle stations. The line of rumbling metal behemoths arcing one-by-one into takeoff position, we watched our predecessors align. The four engines pre-takeoff, run up full throttle, had the banyan leaves dancing taut behind us. We followed in this strange and eerie cadence. Then the creeping rumbled louder as we gained speed and lifted—not into any wild blue yonder, but the dark sky above. Our rapture now was "needle, ball and airspeed" and a compass heading for Ballale air strip an adventure none of us had ever imagined.

En route, it was a kind of quiet, undemonstrative tension—quiet but palpable as we breached daylight and enemy territory and our headsets crackled with a hyper-tenor cry, "Three o'clock." That had to be Staff Sergeant Joe Kerwin at the starboard waist gun spotting incoming Zeros. Our new blue sky was a fish-bowl diorama with a deadly file of Zeros—shark-like escorts out of range of our 50-caliber machine guns, impudently out racing our echelon. But still at three o'clock, one by one the sharks now a hundred yards ahead of us, winged over and closed in, their 7mm tracers burning the starboard sky. Kerwin's 50s respond; it was a staccato baptism of war. We were no longer virgins—now we were engaged!

We landed back on Guadalcanal at Henderson Field, in pitch black at 2345. Thrilled at the excitement of having completed our first combat mission without any difficulty, we chatted all the way back to the barracks. The ground crews took care of Scootin' Thunder, getting her ready for our next combat flight and checking on the faulty racks.

Soon after our landing we got word that Lieutenant Lord, flying El Bastardo, had not returned. His plane had crashed into the sea. Two of his crew, the bombardier and nose gunner, were lost. Lieutenant Lord and the rest of the crew swam to the surface in about 30 feet of water. They swam halfway to shore and were picked up by natives who fed and lodged them for the night. The following day a Navy PBY (Patrol Bomber Aircraft) picked up the eight crew members and brought them home. The navigator, Lieutenant Roark, was taken to the hospital.

In one of our first briefings we were given information about some of the surrounding islands in the Solomons. We were told that Malaita and some areas of Munda were known to have head-hunters. In the event our plane should crash we were told to stay clear of these islands. There were several islands that welcomed any U.S. soldiers and would provide food and lodging until the crews could be rescued. Some of these inhabitants were so badly treated by the Japanese that they welcomed our servicemen with open arms. However, you would never see any of the women. It was always men and young teenage boys. They hid the women on the island away from all other men.

Our survival kits included laminated cards with a sort of Pidgin English so that we could communicate with the locals. We were all well aware of the danger we would face if we were captured by the Japanese. They did not observe the Geneva Convention and were known for torturing and beheading U.S. servicemen. In most instances they would mutilate the bodies, eat the flesh from the thighs and cut open and remove the liver and serve it as a delicacy to their officers.[1]

This was one of the reasons that all U.S. officers carried a .45 automatic at all times on all missions. It was part of our uniform and just a way of life in our now hostile surroundings. I only hoped I would never have to use it. I'd had practice training with it and was not at all pleased with my inability to hit my target. I was just glad we didn't have the broad side of a barn as a target or I'd really have been embarrassed. Fitz, having grown up in Texas, and having done some hunting as a kid, was more adept at handling his weapon. We didn't have much use for guns growing up in Logansport, Indiana. I suppose while Fitz was hunting, I was spending my time reading books, listening to classical music, going to the movie

---

1. Many Americans did not know about this. See two books by: Witts,David. *Forgotten War, Forgiven Guilt*. Las Cruces, New Mexico:Yucca Tree Press.2003. Bradley, James. *Fly Boys, a true story of courage*. Back Bay Books 2003.

theatres and working as a stringer for the Logansport newspaper. It was all good fun and had been such an innocent time just a few years before.

We had the following day off but were about to meet the man who would have a profound influence on us for the rest of the war and years to come. He brought together a lot of young individual-thinking boys and challenged them to think and act as a team and become men.

Chapter 4

June 18, 1943 Friday

Our scheduled briefing for our next mission took place at 1600 hours. We were to meet on the airfield near one of the parked planes. I saw several crew members from the squadron standing around talking when a major and another officer approached the group. Everyone stood at attention when the officer was introduced. "Gentlemen, this is Lieutenant Colonel Marion Unruh. He will be conducting the briefing for tonight's mission." The Colonel stood 6 feet tall and had dark brown hair with clear blue eyes. He was all of 32 years old, which seemed quite old to me at the time, he being ten years older than myself. He told us to have a seat and everyone immediately sat down on the hard dirt field.

We formed a huge circle around the Colonel and listened intently as he described, in a very somber and distinct tone, our combat mission for that night. This man was no nonsense and spoke in a matter-of-fact style, never smiling. He told us we would be taking off at 1820 hours to raid the Kahili airfield on Bougainville. He turned slowly as he described our duties, making sure he made eye contact with each individual. There was no mistaking, he was in charge and he was going to fly lead plane to Kahili with us. I admired his style right away and so did the other men. He could have remained behind in the comfort of his own quarters, awaiting the results of the mission in a debriefing from the first pilots. That was not his idea of leading men. He set the example for all of us by being and remaining out front, participating along with the entire squadron. Colonel Unruh would be piloting his plane, the Pretty Prairie Special, and Scootin' Thunder would be flying on his left wing.

Our eager young crew was on board as Fitz took us off the ground at 1820 hours, just after the Colonel. The planes were carrying 40 fragmentation cluster bombs each. We were to rendezvous over Cape Alexander and from there we flew in formation coming in at a northeasterly direction. Our altitude was 15,500 feet. Visibility was good. Only 10 planes in our squadron took off and only seven made it over the target. I looked at my watch and it was 2110.

Six to eight searchlights caught us over the target and we could see the flak exploding all around us. The searchlights stayed on us for a minute and a half when Garman said, "We're right over the target, Fitz."

Fitz said, "Okay Junior, it's all yours."

For just a few minutes Junior Harris had control of the plane as he sat hunched over his Norton bomb sight. "Bombs away," shouted Junior.

Then Garman shouted, "Do a 180 and get the hell out of here."

Other ships from the squadron followed suit and dropped their bombs in succession. The squadron managed to get 220 of the frag bombs released onto the airfield below. We were on our way home when Fitz had some difficulty with his oxygen system and told me to take over. He pulled the mask off and got out of his seat and positioned himself on the floor space between our seats. He was shivering but said he was OK. His oxygen line was broken, making him groggy.

We took the same route home and noticed the overcast in the weather over Choiseul. As we got closer to home we dropped in altitude and Fitz returned to his seat, taking us in for a landing at 0110. Our second combat mission successful and completed, we headed for our bunks exhausted.

June 19, 1943 Saturday

Fitz and Billy G got up this morning to go for a swim. I opted for more sleep. Our briefing for tonight's mission began at 1500. The target was, once again, the Kahili airfield. Ten B-24s from the 72nd Squadron were scheduled to take off from Henderson Field at 1830 hours. The first four ships were led by Major Sansom in his plane, Laden Maiden. The other ships were Huggermugger, flown by Lieutenant O.G. Adams, My Baby Bub, flown by Lieutenant Frampton and Mary Lou, flown by Lieutenant Gerald Cass. They would lead the attack on the airstrip at Kahili.

Colonel Unruh led the second element of three planes in the Pretty Prairie Special. Scootin' Thunder was on his right wing and Lieutenant John Grace flew the Spirit of Lakeland on his left wing. The third element was led by Captain Riggs in his plane, Big Chief. On his wings were Lieutenant Barclay in Geronimo and Lieutenant Burke flying The Shadow.

Our altitude coming over the airfield was 14,200 feet. It was almost a repeat of the previous night, dropping our bombs at 2110 while in formation. Our bomb racks stuck halfway down and Junior Harris hit the salvo handle releasing the rest of the bombs. However, tonight we managed to drop 310 bombs on the airfield, starting several fires that were visible for 60 miles out. We did encounter some searchlights and some anti-aircraft fire, which was below the altitude of our planes.

On the return flight Garman said, "Houser, give us some songs." I knew the crew felt relaxed after the raid so I sang several songs for the long flight home. This got to be a habit and was a way for all of us to settle down after all the adrenalin flowing during combat. We returned to Henderson airfield landing at 2345, tired but excited about the visible damage we inflicted on the enemy.

June 23, 1943 Wednesday

The crew was prepared to take our plane over to the Carney airfield about 10 miles from the Henderson Field. Fitz had met with one of the ground crew officers; a guy named Yeager who told him they had found five oxygen leaks in the system and fixed all of them. This was of little consequence when you consider we nearly crashed on takeoff. We didn't get the ship up high enough to clear the trees so Fitz flew in between the trees at the end of the runway. The guys in the back of the plane missed the excitement and I held my breath as Fitz guided this huge bomber with its 110 foot wingspan through the banyan trees as if he did this all the time. We landed just fine and attended the briefing for the mission to Buka. It was another early evening because our takeoff was scheduled for midnight. It was later called off due to the weather.

June 24, 1943 Thursday

We had the morning off and Fitz went for a swim with another first pilot, Lieutenant Williams. Later in the afternoon the horseshoe games started. Garman and I were undefeated as Fitz and Williams challenged us. We won and remained the champions. At 1730 we attended another briefing and then came back to the hut to play some records. Some of us got some rest for a few hours then we proceeded to the mess at 2300 for a quick bite to eat before our scheduled takeoff at 0030.

June 25, 1943 Friday

The Buka Passage was our next target. Buka Island is just north of Bougainville and our orders were to strike in the early morning hours with the main objective being the airdrome. Nine planes took off with Scootin' Thunder being in the third element. Our takeoff time was 0152 as we climbed to an altitude of 17,000 feet. At 0349 the bomb bay doors were opened and Junior shouted, "Bombs away".

Seven planes made it over the target area. We dropped our load hitting between the shoreline and the runway. In total, 198 frag cluster bombs made their mark on the passageway below. Again we surprised the enemy and made a turn for home, dodging some isolated thunderheads on the way back. Fitz caught some sleep on the way home after only having an hours rest before this morning's takeoff. We landed at 0630 and Scootin' Thunder made a perfect touchdown just as the sun was beginning to rise.

The ground crews were just coming to life and surrounded the returning Liberators to prepare them for the next mission. We, on the other hand, were looking for the trucks to drive us back to our bunks and some much needed rest.

The following day we got some rest and a few changes were made regarding sleeping arrangements. All the first pilots were assigned to one Quonset hut and Fitz had to pack his things and move to the other barracks. It wasn't far away at all. However, I supposed for debriefing sessions, they wanted all the first pilots together. Fitz still came over to spend as much time as he could with us; after all, our crew was like brothers.

After each combat mission the officers were given an ounce of whiskey if they wanted it. Garman, Fitz and I decided to save our shots in a bottle until we were able to fill it to the top; Junior had other ideas with his share. That Saturday night, June 26th, we had another briefing at 1730 for our next mission. Afterwards, we went to the mess tent for dinner and back to the barracks for some letter writing and bull sessions. We made it an early lights out so that we could get a few hours of sleep.

It was 0200 when Fitz woke me with, "Hey Houser, get up! We have a raid on Kahili this morning." Being a night person, I never figured out how he could have so much energy first thing in the morning. The crew was up, dressed and fed and out to the airfield by 0245. Our takeoff was set for 0300. It was cold and dark but the crew came to life as they assembled and got on the plane. Homer "Red" Noland is our nose gunner and John Mattson our tail gunner. When Fitz and I jumped down from the truck I was greeted with, "Morning, Lieutenant."

I responded with, "Good morning guys, I hope you've had your coffee." Our waist gunners, Staff Sergeant Tom Jones and Joe Kerwin, were checking out their gear. Donaldson Gorsuch, our crew chief and top turret gunner, was talking to our radioman, Leo Wainman. All these guys were a great bunch of young kids except for Wainman. He was the old man at 35 but a hell of a nice guy always talking about his wife, Hon. The early morning hour didn't seem to faze them and I actually enjoyed the excitement of our pending raid.

Chapter 5

June 27, 1943 Sunday

Fitz took Scootin' Thunder down the runway and lifted off at 0300 right on schedule. We climbed to an altitude of 18,000 feet and were over the target and bombs away at 0510 hours. The visibility was poor and only four planes made it over the target area. We were met by two to five searchlights scanning the skies for us. In total, we dropped 145 bombs and headed for home. We touched down at 0730.

One of the men from the ground crew took a picture of our guys in front of Scootin' Thunder. Each of us held up five fingers for completing our fifth raid. We had shot down five Zeros in the past 10 days. Then we were off to breakfast.

Our nose gunner, Homer "Red" Noland, was a young kid from Kansas City, Missouri. Red was a quiet guy but always ready with a smile. However, when he was at his guns in the nose turret he took his responsibilities very seriously. Often times when we were returning from a combat mission some of the crew sat in the back relaxing and talking while the others kept a sharp lookout for the enemy. Red spent some of his quiet time writing poetry. One morning our crew had been eating breakfast when Noland reached into his jacket pocket and removed a tablet. He tore off the page and folded it in half and handed it to me.

Red said, "Let me know what you think, Lieutenant."

I asked him, "Do you mind if I read it out loud?"

"Sure, that's OK with me," was his reply. I opened the folded page and read the following to our crew:

The Liberators
By Homer Red Noland 1943

Our mighty bombers flew along on high
Soaring by in the clear blue sky.
Echelon after Echelon roared on through
Toward their target with a job to do.

Every plane held ten brave young men
And everyone had a war to win.
Loaded with death for the enemy's lair
And upon arriving they'd wreak despair.

> Cold and miserable they wouldn't quit
> Until on the Japs their bombs had lit.
> Gunners were wary and on alert
> Ready to protect if death should flirt.
>
> Fighter protection above serenely flew
> To knock out any Japs who wouldn't let us through.
> Bombardiers tense were adjusting their sight
> Because their bombs had to land just right.
>
> Steady! Suddenly! There comes a bombs away
> And for hours it seems you begin to pray.
> Flak is bursting in black balls of smoke
> Reminds you that this is no means a joke.
>
> From below there comes a rumbling roar
> And you think for awhile of bloody gore.
> But tensioned nerves release as minds go free
> And tomorrow you'll be ready for another spree.

It never ceased to amaze me what kinds of creativity can come from stressful situations. Noland was one of the men in our first line of defense perched in the nose turret with two .50-caliber guns, writing and expressing his thoughts so poignantly. I said, "Red, do you mind if I keep this?" "Not at all Lieutenant, keep it for your journal." The crew nodded in agreement and complimented Red on his poetry.

June 28, 1943 Monday

We had the day off and spent the morning swimming and pitching horseshoes. Some of the guys went down to the beach for a football game. Fitz and some of the first pilots drove over to the Fighter II airstrip. I stayed behind to catch up on some letter writing. We had the phonograph playing some classical music, which was a nice change of pace and proved to be very calming and relaxing.

As I listened to the music I was thinking how quickly some things had changed in my life. I had finished a year at Drake University in Iowa before returning to Indiana. I had wanted, very badly, to join the Army Air Corps but needed my mother's signature because I was underage. When I turned 21 on

November 7th 1941, just a month before Pearl Harbor, I enlisted. My mother wasn't pleased with my decision yet realized her days of making decisions for me were over. I was sure she would have rather seen me stay safe in Indiana where I was working for the Logansport Press as a reporter.

June 29, 1943 Tuesday

The day began with a 0800 briefing for a huge daylight raid that was being planned for Kahili. The plan was for 27 bombers and 72 fighters consisting of P-38s and F40s to assemble over the Russell Islands at 1430 and bomb at 1600. The bombers would be carrying 500-pound demolition bombs with instantaneous, 6 hour, 12 hour and 36 hour fuses. If the bombs didn't explode on impact they would within their predetermined fuse settings. We would fly at an altitude of 23,500 feet before releasing the munitions. However, the mission was cancelled due to the bad weather. Billy G and Fitz had some squabble and were arguing about something but quickly dropped it and all was forgotten.

July 1, 1943 Thursday
Daylight raid on Kahili

Two days ago we had a briefing in the operations Quonset hut. A mass operation was in the works with the 72nd Squadron—394th Group and a couple of squadrons from the 307th group. Our initial point or I/P would be Ballale and each plane would be carrying 12 500-pound bombs. Major Sansom would fly in the lead plane.

Fitz and I were doubtful, with all this added weight, about clearing the wires at the end of the runway, but pulled our ship just clear of the obstacle. Scootin' Thunder creaked and groaned as we took off at 1030 and then circled over Cactus until all nine ships of the 72nd got into formation. We joined the 27 other B-24s flying formation over the Russells then headed out for Ballale.

Along the way, 72 fighters, consisting of P-38s and F40s, came alongside and escorted us to the target area. It was a relief to see the F4U Corsairs, called "Whistling Death" by the Japanese and P-38s weaving from one side to the other creating a protective cover for the bombers. Colonel Matheny passed over Ballale and failed to drop his bombs. Our altitude was 23,500 feet as we flew on to Kahili. The cold was almost unbearable, especially for the waist and tail gunners, at -10 degrees. The plane seemed very sluggish due to the extreme cold.

Garman confirmed our location and Junior Harris was given control or our ship as he sighted and then declared, "Bombs away" at 1320. When the bomb bay doors opened you could feel and hear the rush of cold air through the plane. The bombs fell away and the plane automatically recoiled upwards, relieved of its weight. I glanced out the window of the cockpit to see our New Zealand fighters hanging just off our wing. The P-38 fighters were another story. They took off after incoming Zeros, challenging their audacity to interfere with our mission.

Our flight back to Guadalcanal was uneventful and I relieved Fitz so he could go to the back and get some grapefruit juice and chocolate bars that the crew stashed on board. He was still having some difficulty with his oxygen mask, which didn't fit properly. Ice was a rare commodity on Cactus and we discovered that once we were over 10,000 feet the cans of grapefruit juice would become chilled and promise a quenching delight after a heated encounter. The crew relaxed and I finished my song as we came in for a landing at 1610.

July 4, 1943 Sunday

The weather was still very poor and we were on a one-hour alert but were given some time off to attend church. At dinner time we were told the mission was called off so we drove over to Carney airfield to visit with some of the other crews. We returned at 1730 in time for supper and another briefing. It looked as though the mission had been rescheduled for the next day when we would really hit the Japs.

The surrounding areas by our huts were very muddy; at least ankle deep, and the bugs and mosquitoes were a real nuisance. Fitz looked as if he had the measles with all the bites. It was very difficult to ever get really comfortable on this island. When you are just so exhausted and fall asleep on your cot you don't feel the insects biting—or don't care.

July 5, 1943 Monday

Four days after our previous attack we converged on Ballale for another daylight raid. At 1600 we took off in the drizzling rain carrying a payload of 10 500-pound bombs. This time Scootin' Thunder was the last ship on the right flank of the formation. We climbed to an altitude of 18,000 feet even though the weather was heavy with many clouds and thunderheads. Eight planes made it over the target releasing 70 bombs on Ballale, 10 on destroyers and 10 more on Munda at 1820 hours. Numerous fires erupted as we blasted the hell out of Ballale.

As quickly as the bombs released, Garman shouted his famous words, "Do a 180 and get the hell out of here." Out of nowhere 15 to 20 Zeros jumped us from the sun and clouds to our right. The other enemy fighters called Zekes and Haps put us in a running flight at 200 mph. It was a typical Zero attack over our lower starboard front quarter. They were flying out of range parallel, climbing and peeling into us, and then they would make a roll out of their bank and split. Tom Jones, in the ball turret, said he felt the flak hitting all around him.

Fitz and I surveyed the sky around us trying to see the direction of the next incoming Zero attack. All the while black and orange puffs of flak exploded all around us. We both spotted our next attacker at the same time.

Fitz shouted, "He's coming in at 1 o'clock. Be ready to take over if I'm hit." I followed the Zero never taking my eyes off him and said, "He's diving and going for engine number 3." Gorsuch was in the top turret and pounded his 50-caliber at the intruder as he missed us completely.

Because of the attack, we broke out of formation after 45 minutes and proceeded with Garman correcting our course to 127 degrees before getting back on track. We spotted the searchlights at Henderson Field and brought her in for a landing at 2045. Scootin' Thunder took the brunt of the attack due to our position, yet she safely brought us all home.

July 6, 1943 Tuesday
The Buka Passage

Mission number eight was a raid on the Buka Passage. Our briefing was on the airfield at 1430. Two squadrons from the 307th were to hit Kahili. Our group and the 394th were given the task of hitting Ballale. In addition to our squadron of B-24s we would have some B-17s flying with us. The planes were loaded with fragment cluster bombs as we took off at 1602. We were flying in the second element and were over the target just before dark at 1900. The bombs fell from 18,000 feet as we managed to get seven ships over the target with 192 bombs leaving their mark.

The explosions from our raid climbed to 1,000 feet as we turned and flew the northern route home through the Manning Strait. I flew in formation as soon as the bombs were away for the trip home. The mood of the crew was cheerful with lots of joking and kidding and Fitz said, "Give us some songs, Bob." Wainman was able to pick up the States on the radio and I accompanied the tunes being broadcast. Singing helped the time go by faster as we waited to see the familiar airstrip of Henderson Field.

We encountered light showers on the way back, landing on Cactus at 2135. All ships were accounted for with the exception of two from the 307th; Lieutenant Don "Hat" Hathaway and his crew and Lieutenant Joe Littlepage and his crew in their ship, Billie B. All were lost. Fitz took the news especially hard and walked away from the rest of us into the darkness. He didn't say anything as he headed towards the beach. Fitz, Hat and Epple had been like the Three Musketeers since cadet training back in Texas. It was never easy to lose a buddy; part of you was lost with their death. My very good friend, Lieutenant Herman Levy, was the navigator on Hathaway's plane. Mark Rifkin was the regular co-pilot but had missed this raid and was the soul survivor of 'Hat's' crew. No one really had time to grieve for any of the men and planes lost. We had to regroup and prepare ourselves for our next mission.

July 7, 1943 Wednesday
Buttons

I had lunch with Lieutenant Gordon Hall today. Gordon and I graduated from cadet training together. He stayed behind the extra three months in Tucson, and became a first pilot, while I opted for immediate overseas action as a co-pilot. Gordie was an exceptional athlete and an accomplished gymnast. He even had his folks send him chalk for his hands so he could continue his training on the high bar that he built back at camp. It was great seeing him and we talked about how the training is not even close to the real thing. We said goodbye and good luck as I headed back to Cactus for another mission.

Chapter 6

July 8, 1943 Thursday
Kahili—night raid.

Tonight was another raid on Kahili but took on a special significance with the true test of Bill Garman's skill as our navigator, which earned him the nickname "Clincher."

    At our 1500 briefing we were informed there would be another night raid on Kahili. We taxied from our revetment to the line awaiting our turn to take off. It was now 1750 as we left and Garman gave us a 310 degree heading for Bougainville. We were flying at 11,000 feet and experienced some very cloudy surroundings. We dropped in a cloud and missed hitting Gerald Cass' plane by 50 feet. Fitz and I were focused on trying to find some landmark to get our bearing while avoiding any other planes trying to do the same. It was very scary being in that cloud and not able to judge your distance to the nearest B-24 doing the same. We were on oxygen the entire time and Fitz was having problems with his mask again.

    It was very easy to become disoriented when you were looking for landmarks and none was visible. Billy G led us around the coastline to Kieta and resorted to dead reckoning to the target. He was focused on his charts and was counting the minutes when he told Fitz,

"Turn left 90 degrees now." He continued counting and then commanded, "Turn left again at 90 degrees." We still couldn't see anything of our target.

    Far off, to our right, searchlights went on. Fitz said, "Garman, you blew it, we missed the runway."

    I chimed in with, "Bill, it's way over there on the right where the searchlights are."

    Garman snapped back, "Stay where you are! Don't change course. You will be right over the target in 20 seconds!" The distant searchlights went out immediately.

    Fitz said, "What's the time, Bob?" I moved my left arm to glance at my wristwatch when the lights came on full force illuminating not only my time piece but the runway directly below us. We were cradled in 15 searchlights for four minutes as we dropped all ten of our 500-pound bombs along the tip of the runway. We were waiting for the ack-ack but it never came. That caused a new fear which meant the Japs probably had night fighters in the air. They could have easily shot us down as our vision was hindered by the searchlights.

After a sigh of relief, we flew back to Cactus with Billy G guiding us home. Fitz put on the AFCE (Automatic Flight Control Equipment) and got out of his seat and sat on the floor beside me trembling and exhausted. Thanks to his stubbornness, once Bill Garman locked on to a thought or took a position in a discussion, he clinched onto that thought and could not be swayed. We tagged him with a new nickname, "Clincher." The guy is stubborn as all get out but more often than not is right. On the way back home I sang "Night and Day" by Cole Porter...another guy from Indiana.

The crew was growing stronger, working like a football team. The gunners were very protective, keeping a sharp lookout while giving Fitz and me more time to focus on the target ahead of us. I could see the rapid evolution of our crew and had come to realize...I now had nine other brothers.

July 11, 1943 Sunday
Kahili Raid

The briefing began at 1730. We were hitting Kahili again and again to weaken the Japanese stronghold. All of the boys on our crew were ready and waiting for our turn to take off at 1940. The squadron climbed to 15,000 feet. We managed to get only seven B-24s and five B-17s over the target. Junior peered through his scope and exclaimed, "Bombs away" at 2002. The airfield was lit by 22 searchlights focused on us as our bombs slammed into the ground below. The squadron succeeded in getting 354 bombs pounding down the runway. We peeled off and Fitz steered Scootin' Thunder for home.

The weather was dark and treacherous as we made a sharp diving turn at 310 mph to avoid running into a huge thunderhead. The conditions worsened and we had to use instruments to find our way home. At 0015 we brought our ship in for a landing, touching down and taxing to an empty shelter off the runway. The ground crews met us as we shut down all engines and departed. Their night shift was just beginning.

These mechanics and crew hands were an amazing bunch. They worked around the clock, day and night, in all types of weather, to fix broken engines, change blown out tires, mend gaping holes in wings, replace bullet-riddled props and repair and tune engines just in time for our next mission. All these guys performed miracles on our damaged planes day after day. Their skill and perseverance was just another example of their dedication to keep us out of harm's way as best they could. Back in the barracks we made a stencil to paint a bomb on the side of the plane, one for each raid.

July 16, 1943 Friday
Kahili Night Raid

I had never been a superstitious person but we were about to take off on our 13th combat mission and some of the guys on the crew seemed a bit on edge. Our briefing for the night's raid was at 1700. However, our takeoff was delayed until 2120. We were several miles from base when we had a break in our high pressure oil line to the number three engine that controls the planes hydraulics. I immediately feathered the prop, which turns the blade to lessen the wind resistance, and Fitz turned our ship back and headed for home. We were in a condition: code red. The runway lights on Cactus were turned on just long enough for us to land. Everyone got very quiet as Fitz brought Scootin' Thunder in for a safe landing.

We shut down all the engines as Gorsuch hit the bomb bay handle which opened the flexible roll-up doors of lightweight aluminum. We made an even quicker exit through the bomb bay in the event she might catch fire. The ground crews were all around us with fire extinguishers at the ready. We missed the bombing and heard from the others on their return, that they got 369 bombs over the target while 8 to 12 searchlights scanned the sky. We hit our bunks at 0230 relieved to be back and safe for the night.

July 17, 1943 Saturday

We had dinner with some P-40 pilots. They told us about escorting the 307ths B24s in the previous day's raid on Kahili. One P-38 pilot was lost and they took out 40 Zeros and sank three Jap vessels, cruisers and destroyers. One B-24 tail gunner was killed. We told them how our number three engine was about to explode and it was a good thing that we turned back against Fitz's initial wishes. There was an air raid tonight and 27 Japanese bogey bombers came through. Three of them were taken down by our night fighters. Our men on the ground let loose with the 90mm guns with a full moon serving as a backdrop. From my fox hole I occasionally peeked out to take pictures of the surrounding bursts pounding into the sky sounding like thunder.

July 18, 1943 Sunday

Scootin' Thunder is getting a new third engine change. We missed a daylight raid. Fitz went up with Gerry Cass as the cameraman and Gorsuch flew with Lieutenant Wicker. Cass' plane, Mary Lou, was having engine trouble and they had to turn back for home. Fitz told me the fighters really had a field day up there. They got 16 or 17 Zeros and only one P-40 was lost and our pilot was safe. He said this raid blew the hell out of the runway.

July 20, 1943 Tuesday

Several Japanese bogey bombs hit Henderson Field Monday night. We had another briefing at 1730 for our next raid on Kahili. We hoped Scootin' Thunder would be ready to go by then.

Chapter 7

July 21, 1943 Wednesday
Espiritu Santo—Buttons

I just got word that my classmate Lt. Gordon Hall was killed at Buttons today. He was buzzing the field when his prop hit a tree. The report was that his wing broke off and the plane crashed onto the runway. His crew of 10 and two passengers all died in the crash. That was stupid and senseless. I just saw him two weeks ago.

Tonight we saw Artie Shaw's orchestra perform live on stage "Begin the Beguine." Junior was able to get hold of 30 lbs. of ice, so we made ice cream for the crew. Clincher had been drinking a bit too much and began speaking German. When he's drunk, no one can understand him, so we just laugh which causes even more of the harsh diatribe. Bill Garman and I got along great. He was a very bright guy with a good education. He had taught math at the University of Oklahoma. Bill liked good books and music and liked to get into recreational discussions on navigating. Bill didn't suffer fools well. When he became very exasperated he usually resorted to speaking in German. Fortunately for the crew, we only heard this a few times, usually after several drinks. For the most part Bill was smart, reliable and always upheld his responsibilities as our navigator to the fullest. We often called him Billy G and our other Bill—Harris—was affectionately called "Junior," a moniker assigned to him by Billy G.

July 22, 1943 Thursday
Daylight raid on Kahili Shipping

We are awake at 0500. The 72nd will be flying with the 307th and 60 fighters in another daylight raid on Kahili. This time, our I/P (Initial Point) target was the shipping area. At 1345 we took off and circled the Russells awaiting the rest of the squadrons. We flew in formation at 21,000 feet. The bombs were released at 1550 after which, 25 of the Navy's SBDs (bombers) and 30 TBFs (water landing search planes) went to town. There were several near misses.

The Liberators dominated the target by getting 60 500-pound bombs, hitting their mark. We turned for home and when there was no response from the Japs, the P-40s rolled away home. Fitz buzzed the field while in formation as we came in for a landing at 1740.

July 24, 1943 Saturday
Briefing on the Munda Raid

Everyone knew that something very big was about to happen. We had been gearing up for this next raid which would really knock the enemy senseless. Colonel Unruh called the meeting outside near one of the revetments at 1700. There were probably 50 of us sitting around when Unruh walked forward. He was wearing shorts and a T-shirt and it all seemed so casual until his message came across loud and clear.

The Colonel walked briskly to the center of the circle and began the briefing in his normal somber tone.

"Gentlemen, we have an important mission tomorrow morning. There are 18,000 American troops located southeast and northeast of the Munda airstrip. We need these Marines to capture this airfield and they need us to come in and soften the resistance they have been experiencing. These troops will be 600 yards from the target area. We will be coming in at 8,000 feet and as low as 500 feet if necessary. We may lose some people."

The message was matter-of-fact, without emotion, as we all sat quietly and tried to absorb what we were just told.

B-24s are high-altitude bombers and coming in at 8,000 feet or lower can be suicidal. The Colonel said he would be flying lead on this early morning raid. Scootin' Thunder would be on his wing and the bombing would begin before 0700.

"If needed, we will fly two missions tomorrow hitting Biblio Hill, west and north of the landing strip where heavy artillery is located. We will complete the first attack, return, re-fuel and re-arm and carry out a second raid on Munda."

Unruh said we would be accompanied by two groups of B-25s from the 42nd Squadron, two squadrons from the 5th group, 130 SBDs and TBFs, two squads of B-24s from the 307th, all of the 72nd's B-24s and the 23rd Squadron of B-17s.

More than 300 bombers would be attacking the Munda airfield. We would also have the services of nearly 100 fighters providing cover over the target with P-38s, P-39s, and F-40 Wildcats. All of the bombers would be carrying 40 fragmentation cluster bombs. Unruh said we would rendezvous over the Russells and pick up another squadron before heading to Vella Lavella. Once there, we would assemble at 8,000 feet and meet up with some other squadrons before proceeding to the target.

I glanced at some of the other men and they had the same expression. This was damn serious and was going to be a huge display of our air power. Unruh signed off: "Get some dinner and make it an early night. I will see you all right back here at 0400."

He left as quickly as he came and headed back towards the mess tent. The gathering broke up into crews. Guys talked softly and the look of concern was on everyone's face. I watched the interaction and realized some of them were looking back at me as well. Who would survive, who would make it home?

Fitz and I stood by our crew as Garman looked lost in thought. I am sure he was doing some calculations in his head. Fitz broke the mood "Gorsuch," he said, "I want you to make sure our ship is ready. Wainman, give him a hand. All of you check your stations and make sure everything you need is on board. Get some rest and we'll meet at the trucks at 0330."

Everyone proceeded back to the barracks, got some food and milled around. I spent a bit of time updating my journal and writing a letter home. It was now 2130 and lights out. I tried to sleep but the anticipation of what we were about to undertake kept me awake for another hour or so. I lay on my bunk, staring into the darkness, waiting for some much needed sleep. After about an hour of this I quietly got up and went outside. I sat on the steps and lit a cigarette. I could see the faint glow of cigarettes at the steps of other Quonset huts too. I knew it had been very hot on Cactus today, yet I felt a chill I couldn't shake. I went back inside and hit the sack and drifted off to sleep. I wondered what the weather was like in Indiana on this summer night.

Chapter 8

July 25, 1943 Sunday
Munda Point—Daylight raid

"Wake up Houser, we're hitting Munda today!" It was Fitz, rousting me out of bed. I tried to focus and look at my watch—"It's 0245," he said, "Let's get some breakfast." Some of the other men in the barracks began to stir and prepare themselves for the day's events. There was plenty of hot coffee to go with the spam and eggs. The cold early morning air dictated that we would be wearing our jackets on the truck ride to the air field.

At 0330 our crew was waiting at the trucks along with all the other guys for the 20-minute ride to the strip. Timo was carrying enough supplies for four men. He had several canteens, twice as many clips for his .45 automatic and a king-size supply of chocolate bars. The majority of the other crew members carried only a leather jacket and an oxygen mask.

We were scared but the air was not silent and filled with awe. The men were rowdy and talking obscenities and laughing. I knew this was transparent bravado. The big fright was as remote in our thoughts as the possibility of seeing Times Square in the next 15 minutes.

We arrived at 0350 to find Gorsuch and Wainman waiting for us. All the men walked to their planes as if this were just another day at the office. In the darkness the talk was subdued as we climbed on board and went through our check out procedures.

Colonel Unruh and his crew, on the Pretty Prairie Special, taxied to the line, Scootin' Thunder right behind. The night thundered alive with the sounds of dozens of Pratt & Whitney engines coming to life.

We took off at 0430 and circled over the Russells until the squadron assembled. Our next rendezvous point was Vella Lavella as we climbed to 8,000 feet and waited for the other squadrons to fall in line. We kept a sharp lookout as the sunlight was not yet upon us and the sky filled with bombers. This was like some kind of ballet in the sky.

The Colonel led the way, changing course to Munda as we flew left wing. He dropped to 7,700 feet as we approached the island. A glimmer of first light in the east showed we had company, hordes of escort fighters above and around us, as we released our bombs at 0635.

After we unleashed our payload we followed the Pretty Prairie Special as she turned and headed back for the two-hour trip home. We were never more than eight feet from her wing. We could see a line of bombers still cruising into position for their turn to unload their ordnance.

On our return to Henderson Field we flew in a 12-plane vee formation and buzzed the strip. We were back on Guadalcanal at 0810.

The ground crews snapped into action when they saw the approaching Liberators returning from the first mission of the day. We taxied to a revetment and shut everything down. The crews began the task of refueling and rearming each plane as we made the best of the next few hours. All of the fuel had to be hand-pumped from 55 gallon drums into the Liberators. Each plane carried 3,614 gallons of fuel. In addition, the bomb loading was primitive too—no machinery, all by manpower.

We had four hours before the planes would be ready. Most of us went back to the barracks to rest after stopping at the mess tent for a quick lunch. I preferred to go back to the hut to jot down some notes into my journal from our first Munda raid while they were still fresh in my mind.

I headed towards the first pilots' quarters at 1115. Garman and Junior were standing by the official clock to get the correct hack mark to synchronize and check their watches. I was walking up the steps to the first pilots' hut as some of them were leaving. I shouted, "Fitz, let's go," just as he was coming down the stairs. The four of us walked to the trucks together. The rest of our crew, fed, rested and ready to do this all again, climbed onto the truck. We got to the field and all the guys jumped from the truck and walked to their planes.

At the field, my friend, Lieutenant Al "Kahili" Cohen, asked our crew to stand in front of our plane for a quick picture. Since I spent my down time writing I hadn't eaten lunch. Now that we were about to take off for the second mission of the day I was trying to eat a sandwich before heading back to the cockpit. All the lads obliged the budding photographer and posed for the photo. The crews were boarding their ships as we heard some of the B-24s coming back to life with the "pop-pop" of their engine number three warming up.

We learned that General Harmon was on Guadalcanal and would be flying in the lead ship with Colonel Unruh. Our instructions, for the second part of this mission, were to circle Rendova to the north and attack in two five-plane vee formations. The 72nd's were the only bombers that were right on target from the first raid, blowing off 16 feet from the crest of Biblio Hill.

The planes taxied into position. Scootin' Thunder was loaded with frag cluster bombs, as were all the planes in the first element. The ships in the second element each carried 10 500-pound bombs.

After our 1210 takeoff, we followed the Pretty Prairie Special on a 62 degree magnitude heading. We met our escorts at the Rendova rendezvous and came in to Munda at 7,500 feet over the hills. Our fighter coverage was excellent as we followed the lead and dropped our bombs at 1403, blasting the hell out of the hills of Munda and the artillery emplacements. We were back on Cactus at 1615, exhausted and hungry.

July 26, 1943 Monday
Espiritu Santo—Buttons

Lieutenant John Epple and his crew were killed today. We heard that they were coming in for an emergency landing with their third engine on code red. The field was busy with other Liberators landing and the tower told them to go around again. While circling and making their approach, the engine cut out and they crashed into the sea.

John Epple was the first pilot, Lieutenant A. W. Lipkin was the co-pilot, Lieutenant R. Jackson the bombardier and Lieutenant George Sutton, navigator. All were lost. We had just been talking to John yesterday and played a game of horseshoes after dinner. Fitz and John were classmates in cadet training and very good pals. Fitz walked off to be alone when he got the news. I watched him leave the area with his head down. I didn't know what to say to him but figured he wanted to be by himself, so I let it be.

One of the guys is working on our flight jackets today, painting the insignia and B-24 on the back.

July 28, 1943 Wednesday
Daylight Raid on Ballale

Combat mission number 17. I attended our briefing at 1715 along with Fitz, Billy G. and Junior. We would be striking Kahili the next morning with Colonel Unruh leading the way. Our I/P would be Treasury Island which is north and 10 miles closer to Bougainville.

We were up at 0500 for breakfast and onto the trucks by 0600 for the ride to the field. At 0715 Scootin' Thunder lifted off and climbed to 8,000 feet for our rendezvous over the Russells. There we picked up 32 fighters escorts and took the ships up to 24,000 feet. Unruh took us over the runway at 160 miles per hour with 50-feet intervals, all our 100-pound demo bombs slamming into the runway at 1024. We were off Unruh's left wing, on the number three position. I glanced out the cockpit and saw several Navy TBFs and SBDs striking the harbor just six minutes after our initial bomb run.

July 30, 1943 Friday
Ballale Daylight Raid

Today's raid on Ballale began with an 1155 takeoff. The 72nd Squadron has really been the workhorse on these missions. Again, Unruh led our squadron over the Russells where we picked up our escort of 60 fighters. We had P-38s, P-40s and F4U Corsairs providing coverage as we flew across Ballale at 23,000 feet. The visibility was from five to ten miles and we got seven ships over the target. Junior sighted, and then shouted, "Bombs away" at 1452.

Unruh had instructed us to string across the island. However, we came in too close, resulting in heavy flak. We could see the black and orange puffs of smoke popping all around us. We saw several Zeros flying parallel to us but it was a short attack. We saw one Zero hit an F4U Corsair fighter and watched as he careened into the sea. Our fighters far outnumbered them and the Japs kept their distance.

On the way home, Gorsuch approached Fitz announcing, "Lieutenant, it looks like Harris is asleep again in the nose.

Fitz said, "Ok, I'll take care of it." Fitz grinned at me and winked. He clicked on the intercom system and said loudly with excitement in his voice, "Prepare for a crash landing!" Seconds later you could hear Junior hit his head on the overhead. Then Fitz said very calmly…"Junior, do I have your attention?"

A meek reply from our bombardier, "Yeah, Fitz…I'm awake.

"Good, keep it that way," replied Fitz.

The squadron flew home in formation and landed in heavy rain at 1710. The crew exited the plane and everyone walked around Scootin' Thunder looking for damage. We had two holes through our left wing the size of a basketball, one through a flap and one near a tire. Fitz found a slug lodged in one of the props, gouged it out with his knife and dropped it in his pocket. Smiling at me he just said, "Souvenir." We ate a cold supper and hit the sack, our bodies aching from the stress and tension of the mission.

Chapter 9

August 1, 1943 Sunday
Kahili Daylight Raid

The 72nd was going to have two squadrons from the 307th along with 18 SBDs, 18 TBFs and an escort of 48 fighters on our next attack on Ballale. Colonel Unruh, along with Captain Riggs, led the mission as we took off at 1145. Major Sansom rode with us in the number two position just off Captain Riggs' right wing. The fighters were instructed to hit shipping in the Buin Shortland area.

All the B-24s carried 10 100-pound demo bombs and each squadron got seven Liberators over the target. We had one of the best attacks on Kahili unleashing 240 bombs at 1447. I think Clincher was taking movies of the bombs away. Our altitude was 24,000 feet as I looked out to see dust clouds coming off the runway. Jap Zeros taking off like gnats coming up to try to knock us out of the sky.

Heavy flak burst in front and to the left and rear. We had 30 fighter escorts protecting us as we peeled off and returned home, landing at 1710. Scootin' Thunder had made 18 of the squadrons' 21 raids and our crew probably had the best record in the heavy bombardment group.

Tokyo radio broadcast about a week before that there wouldn't be an American soldier alive on Guadalcanal after today. In fact today was supposed to be our last raid for this stint and we would go to Buttons (Espiritu Santo) soon!

I'd noticed a change in Fitz; he had a sort of, "What the hell" attitude. I knew he was a wonderful pilot but I was concerned that this war was eating him up with grief. It seemed that he wanted to spend more time alone. I kept an eye on him and resolved to try talking to him when we had some time away from the plane.

August 5, 1943 Thursday
Rekata Bay—Daylight Raid

Mission number 20 got underway off Henderson Field at 0920. We were to join two squadrons of the 307th headed for Kahili. We came in at 9,500 feet. The lead bombardier sighted short on the peninsula target and half his bombs hit the water. Junior Harris sighted independently and almost all our bombs hit the target at 1201. We started calling Junior, "Sweet William, The Murderer."

The squadrons from the 307th made a right turn and headed back home. However, the 72nd experienced heavy automatic fire and cut its right turn short and stopped on a heading to Rekata Bay without fighter cover. At 15,000 feet we noticed ice forming on our wings. Fitz descended and headed for Vanganu Island. We landed at Carney Field on Guadalcanal at 1500. There was a big blow out party with plenty of food, beer, candy and hamburgers.

We completed our 20th combat mission today, hitting Vella LaVella. The weather had been very bad with thunder clouds and hard rain by the time we landed. It seemed odd to me that Fitz could feel so jittery on the ground before a mission but smoothed out when he flew. I guessed he was just a natural-born pilot.

Prompted by rumors that 25 combat missions would get us a ticket home to the States, Billy G, Fitz and I decided to approach the topic with a Major who scheduled the R&R leaves. Instead of a calm discussion we were reprimanded for even asking. The Major lectured, "You will stay as long as needed; after all, there is a war going on and you should not be asking when you can leave. You should be proud to do your duty!"

None of us needed to be reminded that a war was going on around us. We'd seen it first hand on 20 combat missions. Bill Garman asked if the major had any combat flying time. That was a gutsy call considering the tongue-lashing we had just received. The Major answered, "No, but I'll fly the next one to prove my point."

The major went along on our next mission on August 9th. When we landed, the major was one of the first men off our ship. He returned to his quarters without a word. Two days later the major was transferred into a non-combat zone. So much for "doing your duty." I guess the assigned reason for the transfer was a case of hay-fever.

Meanwhile, we heard that Colonel Unruh had gone to the ground crew repair tent looking for Corporal Roy Davenport, one of the exceptional mechanics in the outfit. Unruh, in addition to being a great pilot, had a strong engineering background and we heard was looking for a way to improve the aim of his gunners.

In every spare moment Unruh worked very closely with Roy and told him of a project he had in mind for training gunners. He queried Roy about the possibility of cannibalizing spare parts from the damaged Liberators. Roy took him to a veritable plane graveyard, with parts strewn in so many heaps. Unruh's quest was a turret section that they could end up redesigning for target practice. They designed a scaled-down model of a Jap Zero, suspended within range of their new turret. The Zero would mimic the moves of a real plane by virtue of a motor-driven cam. They tested it several times and were finally able to recreate a mock attack and have gunners sit inside the turret and aim the guns to improve their accuracy. These men worked on this project for several weeks in their spare time. They hadn't yet decided how to make the training guns work.

Chapter 10

August 6, 1943 Friday
Carney Field Hospital on Guadalcanal

Entry of the day—we now had Munda Airfield! 1,681 Japs were killed and 28 prisoners taken during the ordeal.

This morning I had breakfast with the two Williams. Fitz was nowhere to be found. Afterwards, Junior said he wanted to go see some of his Navy buddies about some supplies. Garman and I were headed to the tent that housed a makeshift library to get a few books when we ran into Timo.

Timo said that he and a couple of guys just came back from the beach and were deciding whether or not to go for a swim. The gremlin actually seemed concerned when he said, "I saw Fitz sitting off by himself. He didn't look like he was going to go fishing or swimming. I shouted, 'Hey' to him and he just ignored me. I thought you guys might want to check on him."

Garman said, "Fitz is a big boy, we don't need to baby-sit him. Besides, maybe he wants to be alone for a while."

I said, "Thanks Timo, we'll take a look see." The gremlin waved goodbye and was on his way having done his good deed for the day. I saw a jeep that was available and looked at Billy G and said, "Let's go check it out."

Garman said, "Ah, come on Bob. Maybe he's just getting some fresh air."

I answered, "Yeah, or maybe he's still upset about Hathaway and Epple getting killed. Either way we need to distract him."

Garman agreed with a nod of his head and we both got in the jeep and drove out to the beach. We left the jeep on the dune and walked down to where Fitz was sitting. He didn't hear us coming and had his head down. Bill and I sat down on either side of him and Fitz continued to stare at the sand.

I patted him on the shoulder and said, "Fitz, you don't have any fishing gear and it doesn't look like you're planning on swimming. Are you OK?"

Fitz briefly glanced at me and said, "Yeah, I'm OK." I could see he had been crying.

Bill offered, "It's really peaceful out here away from camp. I can see why you like it." Fitz rubbed his eyes and said, "Sometimes it helps to just get away from the camp and all the noise." He paused for a moment and then said, "Sometimes I wonder if it's all worth it. All these great bunch of young guys crashing and dying for what? How can any of this help us win this war? Guys, I need to be alone."

Bill looked at me and we both stood. I said, "You've had enough time alone, let's go." Bill and I took him under each arm and lifted him to his feet.

"A change of scenery is just what we all need. Brush yourself off and let's go," I commanded. Fitz didn't put up any argument. I think he was exhausted and welcomed the change. We all walked back up to the jeep and drove over to the field hospital at Carney.

The Munda raid happened two weeks ago and I knew there were some casualties at the field hospital. I thought it would do us all some good to visit with the wounded Marines. The three of us walked in wearing our A-2 flight jackets with just the fronts being visible. Four Marines were laid up in bed with various injuries but welcomed the visit from the three of us.

Fitz walked through the door first. "How ya boys doing?" One of the guys answered, "I've had better days, I'm just glad to be out of that gully."

A second Marine asked, "Were you guys in that squadron of bombers over Munda?" Garman replied,

"Yeah, we were right over you, about 600 yards ahead to be exact." Bill shook hands with the Marine and said, "I'm Bill Garman, the navigator, they call me Clincher. That guy there is Bob Houser, our co-pilot, and that young rascal there is our pilot, Oscar Fitzhenry."

I interrupted, "Yeah, he's called Clincher because you'll never win an argument with him. Once he locks on to an idea, he doesn't let go."

A third Marine said, "Boy that was a beautiful sight. I almost cried for joy when I heard all those bombers flying over."

The second Marine chimed in, "Man that was great to see all those bombs dropping from the sky; it sounded like thunder."

I looked over at Fitz and smiled. "Yeah, well we wanted to thank you guys for doing such a great job clearing Guadalcanal for us. We owed you," I replied.

A fourth Marine said, "God, you would never catch me in one of those planes, you guys are sittin' ducks."

I said, "Well, you would never catch me on the ground in some foxhole. Besides, the view is better from a B-24."

The second Marine stated very enthusiastically, "I mean to tell ya, you guys filled the sky with all those bombers and fighters, P-38s and P-40s. Geez, it's like you came out of nowhere and were just scooting along, all over the sky."

Clincher looked at me with a huge grin. "Well, we wanted to make sure we didn't cause your injuries."

The third Marine answered, "Hell no, you saved our asses."

The first Marine asked, "What squadron are you boys with?"

Fitz answered, "The 72nd Squadron, 5th Bomb Group." The same Marine asked me, "What's that patch mean?" pointing to the large round red patch with a skull with wings attached to it on the front of my jacket.

"That's a Hawaiian symbol and saying for 'Guardian of the Heavens.' All the boys in the 5th Bomb Group wear this patch."

Fitz spoke up, "We need to be getting back, we have another briefing tonight."

The third Marine said, "Thanks for the help. I'm sure it was dangerous for you guys coming in that low."

"You boys rest up and get well. It's been nice to meet you guys," said Fitz.

The first Marine asked, "Hey, what if we should run into you again, how will we know you from all those other fly boys?"

I said, with a smile, "How could you guys forget us? Besides, you already know our plane."

The four Marines looked a bit confused. Clincher, Fitz and I wished them good luck and the three of us turned to leave the hospital room. For the first time the Marines could see the name "Scootin' Thunder" on the back of our flight jackets.

I turned to Fitz and said, "I told you it was a good name." The three of us left feeling proud of our contribution to the raid on Munda. Fitz laughed and made a playful grab around my neck. The visit was just what we needed.

Chapter 11

August 9, 1943 Monday
Raid Vila Airdrome

Technically, today's search for Lieutenant Mike Lord and his crew became a combat mission. It was reported that they had gone down over Vella Lavella the day before. We had Colonel Reddoch flying with us on his first combat mission.

Two squadrons of B-24s were to assemble at 5,000 feet over Cape Esperance by 1000. We were met by some F-40 Wildcats and P-38s over the Russells that would serve as our escorts. Our formation was flying at 21,000 feet when we came in over Vella Lavella. We encountered a storm front and turned back to hit our alternate target, the Vila Airdrome supply area, 30 miles south.

The Liberators dropped to 18,000 feet and we released our bombs at noon. The flak bursts were very close as we managed to get seven planes over the target releasing 180 100-pound bombs that damaged the end of the runway, setting it on fire. We had excellent fighter coverage as we turned and headed for home. Henderson Field was in our sight as we came in for a landing at 1314 in heavy rain. No sign of Mike Lord and his crew.

August 10, 1943 Tuesday

We would be leaving Cactus, after eight weeks, and would be heading for Espiritu Santo (Buttons) for a respite from combat. The crew of Scootin' Thunder said farewell to Guadalcanal, for a while, by buzzing the field at 0800. The summary of our missions at Henderson and Carney: 21 combat missions, 19 times over target, 18 bombs away, one search, possibility we got two Zeros in a Ballale raid, started five fires and had explosions on Buka, Kahili and Ballale. We assisted with the two strikes in one day on Munda and we destroyed several planes on the ground. We were more than ready for a break.

When we got back we found John Epple's things in our tent. Fitz said he would take care of them and wished out loud that Hathaway and Epple were still here. The next day we went to see what was left of John's plane. It was nothing but burnt and melted metal.

August 12, 1943 Thursday
Back on Buttons and tent city.

We were on standby for a search mission off Nauru. Lieutenant Barclay and his crew in their ship, Geronimo, were taxiing when they smashed the wingtip. They stopped and had to switch planes. Scootin' Thunder was having some work done on her and we were scheduled to fly Balls O'Fire. Instead, Barclay and his crew took our ship and flew the search mission.

The heat during the day was unbearable, sapping all my energy. I found it difficult to write and keep my focus, so I decided to wait until the evening to finish my letters when it was a bit cooler.

This afternoon, Doc Schindler and Pappy Arana were playing one-man volleyball with a $20 prize for the winner. These guys were playing like their life depended on the outcome. Doc won by one point, exhausted and in serious need of some water.

That night, some of the guys in a neighboring hut were drinking quite a bit when Clincher came in to our hut laughing. I asked him what was so funny. He said some guy was really plastered and stepped outside on the steps of the hut to take a leak. Clincher started laughing at the sight and the guy yelled, "Whatsa matter, ain't you ever seen this done before?" Then he keeled over off the step in a dead faint. Clincher responded, "Not quite like that!" Some of his buddies picked up the drunk guy and dragged him back inside.

I don't know how the conversation started but some of the other guys in the barracks were giving Junior Harris a bad time about acting immature. They claimed he was only 18 or 19 at the most. Junior did look very young but swore that he would be 21 this month. It wouldn't have surprised me at all if he had been 18.

Junior was always getting into some sort of mischief. He and Timo got together and put up a sign on the outside entrance to the first pilots' Quonset hut. It seems Junior thought these guys were snubbing the other officers. The sign read something to the effect: "This hut is reserved for the elite first pilots." Timo and Junior posted the sign on the door then ran. None of us older guys thought much of it anyway. We knew Colonel Unruh wanted all the first pilots together for more efficient debriefing sessions. Some of the guys did pal around together but most maintained their close relationships with their crews.

August 14, 1943 Saturday

Lieutenant Gerry Cass was back from Cactus telling us of the trials and tribulations of the 31st Squadron. Several of their ships had been badly shot up and we would have to give up some of our planes for their upcoming missions. Gerry is the old man at 28 years but is a great guy. He's a first pilot and you can tell he cares a lot about his crew. Gerry named his plane Mary Lou after his wife and often talks about his 7 year old daughter, Ruth Helen.

Our Scootin' Thunder would have to go back to Cactus and be pressed into service. This was a disappointment for our crew and meant we would have to use whatever planes were assigned. Scootin' Thunder hadn't let us down and she was a great plane with a great crew. She had more strikes than any other crew or B-24 in the squadron. It was difficult to have to hand her over to the 31st. All of us hoped that it would only be temporary.

There had been some Jap bogeys getting through at Henderson and they sank a Liberty Ship last night with a torpedo bomb. This had put a lot of guys on notice and on edge. It happened that Colonel Unruh was coming back from a raid on Kahili and was circling the field in a condition red. Colonel Reddoch was at the controls when one of our guys on the ground, thinking it was another bogey, began firing his 90mm guns at the Pretty Prairie Special. He hit their hydraulic system and Colonel Reddoch had Unruh take over the controls and bring her in for an emergency landing.

Unruh did a superb job landing the ship on her nose and left wheel. No one was hurt. However, the gunner was mighty embarrassed. The heat had been awful and I waited for the night time to write.

August 16, 1943 Monday

Today we flew a search mission waking at 0400. We flew 1,600 miles with just sky, clouds and water in view. Our AFCE (automatic flight control equipment) went out so we flew manually.

August 17, 1943 Tuesday

Word had been circulating that co-pilots were to be checked out soon for first pilot positions. With various mechanical problems and crews crashing, they wanted to make sure they have enough pilots in reserve that could take over. I was eager to get the transitional flying time but had to coordinate the allotted training between whomever of the first pilots who were available.

Some of us went to the army commissary and bought several cases of fruit. Our shortwave radio reports we now have Vella Lavella. We also heard that Kahili took a beating yesterday morning when eight Corsairs shot planes out of the Jap traffic pattern. The dawn sweep also had our fighters taking out the control tower.

August 18, 1943 Wednesday

Fitz took out a plane today so that Lieutenant Graham and I could gain some more experience in the pilot's chair. Fitz sat in the co-pilots seat as we took turns. We had good traffic patterns but some raunchy landings. We flew back and landed and had dinner at the Air Group Camp. Afterward we went back to the barracks to read and play some poker. The next morning we were scheduled for another search mission.

August 19, 1943 Thursday

At 0545 we took off on a wet, slick runway. Showers added cold to the gray dawn. About one hour into our search mission, the weather cleared. However, we ran into a few storm fronts 150 miles south of Nauru. We were 50 minutes from home when we sighted Lieutenant John Grace in his ship, The Spirit of Lakeland. As we crossed over Urepapara Island we saw a fire and circled back to investigate. We couldn't make it out and headed for home landing back on Buttons at 1605. Back in the tent it was drinks and talk of women.

August 20, 1943 Friday

If you needed anything, supply wise, all you had to do was ask Junior. He was our scrounger. Junior was always making some deals, mostly with the Navy guys. He managed to soak me for $10 for a box of "Fancy Tales" cigars. He also acquired some sheets for himself and two more boxes of cigars: Phillies.

I'd been doing a lot of reading and writing on our down time in the barracks. Tiemann (Timo) and Garman were knocking themselves out on a navigation problem: how to get a fix from one celestial body, computing position by a great circle solution in reverse. Timo didn't stand a chance against Clincher. The younger navigator was going to be mauled by the older and wiser one. This was somewhat entertaining, but I went back to my book.

Chapter 12

August 21, 1943 Saturday

Fitz and I went out with Lieutenant Scott to get some more transitional flying time. We practiced landings and flew on instruments. I bounced on the second landing. We landed and spent the rest of the afternoon pitching horseshoes and trying to stay cool.

The weather during the day was unbearably hot and muggy. The horseshoe matches and ping-pong games usually began later in the afternoon. We had so much time off between missions that most of the lads appeared to be bored. It could have just been the heat.

Some of the guys dragged their cots out near the bank of the river to get some sun or to just take a nap. Apparently, Timo didn't feel like horseshoes or ping-pong and felt like starting a new game. Fitz, Clincher and I were outside waiting for our turn at horseshoes when Timo got up from his cot and out of the blue said, "I bet I can throw you into the river."

We looked at the Gremlin and Garman said, "Timo, who are you talking to?"

Timo shot back, "Fitz, I bet I can toss you into the river." Fitz laughed and said to the gremlin, "Timo, you've got to be kidding. It's too hot to wrestle and you are too little to make it a fair match." Fitz turned his back to pick up a wayward horseshoe and the gremlin made his move.

He grabbed Fitz around the waist and started pulling him toward the bank just five feet away. Fitz was laughing and almost immediately, overpowered the little guy. Fitz was a very muscular kid and didn't have much trouble freeing himself from Timo's hold.

The guys playing horseshoes stopped and ran over to watch the wrestling match. In a matter of seconds everyone was laughing and cheering on Fitz. Those that had sympathy for the smaller navigator were hooting and hollering for Timo.

The guys were in T-shirts and long pants as the struggle intensified. Timo was battling but wouldn't give in. Fitz grabbed Timo and the little guy broke the hold but fell back on his butt. Fitz reached down and took Timo by the ankles and started pulling him down the bank. Timo flipped himself over and held on to a branch that was protruding from the bank just a few feet from the water.

Fitz was laughing and said, "Come on Timo, you need to cool off." Timo held on to the branch for dear life as Fitz wrapped both his arms around the gremlin's chest and pulled. The crowd on the sidelines cheered louder and louder as Fitz finally broke the hold Timo had on the branch as they both tumbled into the water below.

They were both laughing but Timo looked tired as he started to pull himself up the bank. Fitz grabbed the little guy once more and picked him up and tossed him back into the river for a second drenching. Every one enjoyed the challenge as Billy G helped Timo out of the muddy quagmire. They had both found a great way to cool off but wound up caked in mud and headed for the showers.

August 22, 1943 Sunday

Fitz flew to Tontonta in a B-17 with Lieutenant Mike Lord. Lieutenant Graham was now the first pilot of Lieutenant Burke's crew, flying The Shadow. However, he still needed to be checked out by recently promoted Major Riggs. We were on stand by again for a search mission. The weather was cloudy and cool. It had been quiet that evening so I spent some time updating my notes and writing in my journal.

August 23, 1943 Monday

The barracks came alive at 0400 when we all managed to get dressed and off to breakfast. At 0600 we would be taking off, flying Old Snodgrass. A TBF was lost and we were instructed to search the triangle sector. It was raining when we took off heading to sea between Aoba and Pentecost. The sea was white with foam and waves 10–15 feet high. On our return we used dead reckoning heading back to Buttons. We never found the TBF.

August 24, 1943 Tuesday

We had an air raid this morning at 0230. Some bogeys were circling overhead and our 90mm guns replied firing into the overcast night. The noise from those guns is loud enough to wake the dead. However, Fitz managed to sleep through the ordeal.

August 25, 1943 Wednesday

I would be flying the B-24 Big Chief today to get some more time as a first pilot. In addition to the crew, we had two Negro sailors on board. I am sure this was a deal between Junior and the Navy. All of the engines were on and idling as we taxied towards the strip. Gorsuch approached Fitz in the co-pilot's seat and said,

"Lieutenant, we have 11 chutes on board and 12 passengers." Fitz told him that one person would have to get off. Gorsuch went back to let the sailors know we had one too many on board.

One of the sailors got off and ran headlong into prop number three, beheading him and tossing arms all over the place. Gorsuch tried to stop him and succeeded in stopping the second sailor on his way after his friend. I heard the noise but did not know what happened. It sounded like cardboard in the spokes of a wheel. I looked at Fitz as if to say, "What was that?" He put his head down and covered his eyes. I heard him say, "Oh God, shut it down." The flight was cancelled and a doctor was called to the scene to get the body. Later in the day we heard a B-24 from the 307th had crashed. It was an awful day for everyone on the crew.

Roy Davenport had mentioned that Colonel Unruh had gone back to the repair crew tent this morning and had another officer with him, General Henry "Hap" Arnold. The four star General was the commander of the Army Air Force during World War II, an aviator and a strong advocate for the United States maintaining air superiority. Unruh introduced him to Corporal Davenport and the two men shook hands. They took the General outside to show him the turret trainer they built together and how it worked. After nearly 20 minutes the general shook hands with Roy and told him he was doing a good job, keep it up. The officers left and Roy continued working on the project.

The next morning Unruh returned to the project tent and Roy apologized for not saluting the general the day before having been completely taken aback at his presence. Unruh reassured him that "Hap" thought nothing of it, "forget it!" The two men got back to working on the turret when Unruh said he wasn't sure what to use that would mimic guns for shooting at the target. Roy suggested using water under pressure. The Colonel thought that might work and they began assembling the necessary parts to get it operational. Together they eventually designed a turret with guns that sprayed a steady stream of water under pressure.

August 26, 1943 Thursday

Fitz reported back to us that Lieutenant Jack "Bucky" Stafford had made a crash water landing about 1800 the day before off fighter strip number one; five miles off the coast. Lieutenant Albert Fuller, the radio operator, was lost. Bucky broke his ankle and Lieutenant Joe Kennelly had a badly broken leg, near his hip. The rest of the crew was bruised and shaken.

Lieutenant Ben McCullough stopped by our tent to fill us in on the details. They ran out of gas and feathered the first engine, and then the number two engine quit over 140 kilometers out at sea. After three engines conked out they were forced to feather the fourth and set her down. The windshield broke off and the ship broke in two places. They were picked up two hours after landing in the sea. A Lieutenant Hudson had spotted their craft almost immediately.

I had some transition flight time in Riggs' Big Chief today. Flying in the pilot's seat; I taxied, took off and flew on instruments then set up with the AFCE landing.

We got the bad news that we were to lose "Scootin' Thunder" the next day to the 31st Squadron. We were all sad but had no control over the assignment of planes. There had been several crashes and planes that were being repaired for one problem or another. The crews that were in combat needed all available Liberators and Scootin' Thunder was needed desperately by the 31st.

Chapter 13

August 27, 1943 Friday
Guadalcanal

Again we were up at 0400 and take off at 0600. We were taking Scootin' Thunder to the 31st Squadron at Cactus. Their ships were badly battered from the hot corner of the Kahili business. They also had six or seven raids in 17 days. In the dark, before takeoff, I painted another bomb on each side of our plane marking her 21st combat mission.

The flight from Buttons was uneventful and very low-key. The chatter between the crew was strained at best. All of us were unhappy about having to give our plane to another crew. Bill Garman would occasionally puncture the silence with headings, distance traveled and the approximate landing time.

Fitz looked at me then said, "How about some songs, George Robert?" I normally like to sing ballads but knew the songs needed to be something cheery and silly to change the mood. My last song before touchdown was "Your Feet's Too Big" just to get the guys laughing a bit. We landed at Henderson Field on Cactus at 0910.

We came in for a landing and saw a DC-3 on fire with flames and smoke billowing several hundred feet above. Apparently, this plane had landed less than 10 minutes ahead of us. The ground crews were fighting the fire as best they could as we brought Scootin' Thunder down and steered her away from the wreckage to an awaiting revetment. Our guys took their gear and got off the plane for the last time. We heard the report that 15 people managed to escape the inferno but one unlucky guy that was bed-ridden perished in the crash.

We flew The Jolly Roger back to Buttons and landed by 1530. It seems strange. It's just another borrowed B-24, not ours. We were all hoping this was a temporary assignment and that we would be able to fly our ship again. We'd already come through 21 combat strikes with her. I knew all of the crew was disappointed and sad to have to loan her out to another crew. I hoped they would have as much success with Scootin' Thunder as we did.

August 28, 1943 Saturday
Guadalcanal

This morning we would be flying in Lieutenant Barclay's Geronimo. We were up at 0200 in time for a takeoff at 0330. However, we blew a left tire while taxiing onto the runway. Fitz pulled her off to the side and we slept in the cockpit while the crew changed the wheel.

At 0700 we were able to take off, when Gorsuch noticed a gas leak in the bomb bay. We immediately came back in for a landing. The leak stopped and we took off for Henderson Field at 0745. About 1050 we brought Geronimo in for a landing feeling glad to be back on the ground.

The crew went to the mess tent for lunch. Fitz, Clincher, Junior and I stayed in the "Dallas Hut" with Lieutenant O.G. Adams. We were wondering what happened to Lieutenant Renfro. He had been flying Lieutenant Leo Hunt's Balls O'Fire. He had to go back to Buttons because his number one engine was acting up. He landed at Cactus later in the day.

Garman and I decided to go swimming and Fitz and his cousin, Lieutenant Claude Craft, went to a fish fry. I am pretty sure Junior was off somewhere on the island looking for some items he could swap with the Navy and sell at a profit to some desperate crew member.

August 29, 1943 Sunday
Back to Buttons

It seems, at times, we are nothing more than a shuttle service. Today we would be flying Tim-ber along with eight sets of luggage racks, back to Buttons. We were delayed waiting for a passenger, Lieutenant Maloney. We touched down on Buttons at 1330.

August 30, 1943 Monday

Gerry Cass and his crew had gone down the other day and we were on standby for a search mission to try and locate them. While we waited around, some of the guys and I set up a horseshoe court in front of our tent. Frampton had been promoted to Captain and some of his crew, Lieutenant Purdy and Lieutenant Charlie Konkle, from the neighboring tent, challenged us to a match. This weather and this island started to close in on you with nothing to do.

August 31, 1943 Tuesday

Today is another day of "hurry up and wait." I played a game of badminton with Junior and Doc Schindler. Afterwards we went to the transient officers' mess and then a movie at our outdoor theater.

The 72nd Squadron is being clamped down upon regarding mail censorship. We can say practically nothing now and were told any next offense will be subject to a court-martial. Apparently, some of the men may have been giving too much information on their location in their letters home. The censors for the Army Air

Corps frown on any information that could be intercepted by the enemy. In spite of the available crews, they're squeezing the last bit of work from us. We were scheduled for a search mission the next day in the Nauru sector, 356 degrees to 05 degrees.

It was beginning to rain in the evening as spring in the Solomon's got underway here. Doc said the malaria season would be starting within the next 15 days and we were to take precautions.

Front row L to R: Joe Kerwin, Tom Jones, Homer Noland, Donaldson Gorsuch, and Leo Wainman. Back row L to R: John Mattson, Bob Houser, Bill Harris, Bill Garman and Oscar Fitzhenry.

Houser, Garman and Fitzhenry at White Sands, New Mexico 1943

Houser and Fitzhenry
on Espiritu Santo (Buttons)
1943

Bill Harris "Junior" bombardier on Espiritu Santo

Garman, Fitzhenry, Houser and Gorsuch

Oscar Fitzhenry - Pilot 1943

Bob Houser co-pilot on Scootin Thunder

Oscar Fitzhenry pilot watching for enemy fighters.

Bob Houser co-pilot

Truck ride to Henderson Field, Guadalcanal.

Jones, Noland, Kerwin, Mattson and Houser on Guadalcanal 1943.

June 27,1943 after 5th combat mission.

Top: Bill Garman- navigator and Bob Houser - co-pilot

Homer "Red" Noland   nose gunner

Garman, Fitz, Jones, Gorsuch, Houser and Mattson.

Colonel Marion D. Unruh and the Pretty Prairie Special

Col. Unruh's crew of the Pretty Prairie Special - Unruh second from left in the back row.

Fitzhenry and Timo wrestling by the river

Fitzhenry and Timo in the river

Timo after the wrestling match with Fitzhenry

Fitzhenry after the wrestling match

S/Sgt. Tom Jones waistgunner and Lt. Bob Houser co-pilot

John Mattson tail gunner and Red Noland

Noland, Gorsuch and Mattson

Major Gerry Cass, B-24 Mary Lou

Plane 752, Fuzzy Wuzzy

B-24s Formation Flying 1943

Tail gunners view

Old Snodgrass

Billie B's Crew

Lt J.R. Littlebone - W.Va.
Lt G.L. Goddard - Ohio
Lt J.H. Scholl - Texas
Lt L.B. Conway - Wash
T/Sgt H.H. Juster - S. Dak.
S/Sgt H.D. Denison - S. Dak.
T/Sgt C.B. Cluff - Utah
S/Sgt C.H. Mulhausen - Okla.
S/Sgt Wm. Posladni - Ohio
S/Sgt T.K. Brady - Ind.

Tucson, Ariz.
Alamogordo, N.M.
Clovis, N.M.
Topeka, Kan.
Overseas
April 2, 1943

Eight crew members of the Pretty Prairie Special found on the beach on December 31, 1943.

Colonel Marion Unruh accepts sword from a Japanese officer when the POW camp was liberated in September 1945.

Bob and Elsa Houser's wedding day
December 31, 1944   Indiana

1990 Reunion on the Queen Mary in Long Beach, CA.
Bill Garman, Bob Houser, Oscar Fitzhenry and Bill Harris.

Bob Houser, Roy Davenport and Oscar Fitzhenry May 2005.
San Diego, California.

Bob Houser's New A-2 Flight Jacket

5th Bomb Group Reunion in San Diego, CA. May 14, 2005
Bill Harris, Bob Houser and Oscar Fitzhenry.

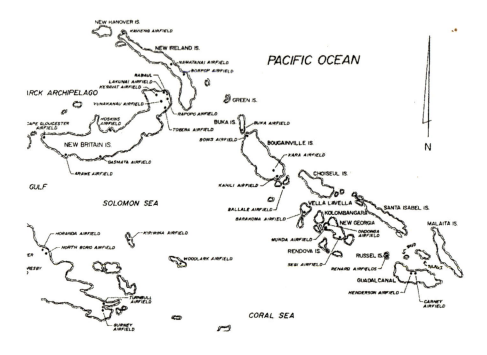

Chapter 14

September 3, 1943 Friday
Auckland, New Zealand

All the crew had been anticipating our much needed leave as we took off from Buttons at 0315 in a C-47 Skytrain named Phyllis. These C-47s could carry 28 passengers or 18 stretchers and had a crew of three men. The Skytrain was a two engine all metal monoplane that flew close to 185 miles per hour. At 0625 we landed at Tontouta for coffee and doughnuts at the Red Cross. At 0700 we took off again headed for beautiful civilization and arrived in Auckland, New Zealand, at 1400.

It was chilly enough for cattle to be wearing blankets. Sheep dotted the hillside as I noticed a golf course that blossomed into view. The air was crisp like autumn as I looked into the faces of the British inhabitants and their florid faces.

We had a briefing at the Dilworth Building, a headquarters for soldiers coming into New Zealand, and then sought out lodging at a commercial hotel. We drew our rations and exchanged our money. One British pound equaled $3.24 in U.S. money. Junior Harris met a gal named Kathleen at tea and invited her to a movie. The boy is a fast worker. Garman and I roamed around the city as Junior and his girl went to a dance at the Civic auditorium. Garman and I made arrangements to get in a round of golf for the next morning.

We got word that Corporal Roy Davenport had been working in the repair tent when a detonator from a hand grenade exploded in his left hand. He was taken to the 39th General Hospital in New Zealand for a recovery time that would last five months. We were the lucky ones to be able to have some time off from combat and experience these beautiful surroundings in Auckland and not from a hospital bed.

September 4, 1943 Saturday

Fitz and Clincher had breakfast together. It was a welcome sight when you consider that Fitz had been very sick for the past three days with food poisoning. While we are here in Auckland, Fitz was still having some difficulty with breathing. When our planes are flying at 10 thousand feet and above we would have to put on our breathing masks and Fitz was still having problems. The doctors have confirmed that Fitz needs to have some surgery on his nose.

September 5, 1943 Sunday

I went to church on the hill with Fitz. It was a Baptist church but we didn't seem to mind. Later in the evening we met Billy G for dinner.

September 7, 1943 Tuesday

Fitz had surgery on his nose. Billy G and I went to visit him in the evening. He was all bandaged and his eyes were covered shut too. Bucky Stafford also stopped by to check on Fitz. We knew he was getting great care at this hospital in Auckland. Too bad he had to spend all this time in bed. I knew once he was feeling better he would make up for lost time.

September 8, 1943 Wednesday

Garman and I went back to the hospital to see how Fitz was doing. Bucky Stafford, one of his good friends, was already there waiting on him. The poor guy needed some help with his head, eyes and nose wrapped like a mummy.

September 13, 1943 Monday
Leave was over.

At 0900 we left Auckland, N.Z., headed for Tontouta, New Caledonia. Fitz would stay behind until September 23rd due to the operation and his recovery needs.

The rest of us went on to Norfolk Island where we landed to refuel. There was much anticipation of rough weather ahead. We arrived in New Caledonia at about 1630. The mood had changed dramatically from the beauty of New Zealand back to the uncertainty of combat.

Junior contacted the flight surgeon complaining of an earache. He was grounded and hospitalized. Garman and I took a bag to him at the hospital where he expected to be a week.

September 14, 1943 Tuesday
On to Espiritu Santo

We were up for breakfast at Tontouta and caught our flight. However, the flight gyro didn't work in the plane so we landed for repairs. At 1230 we were in the air again landing on Buttons at 1540. I spent the rest of the day reading mail and sending some V-mail home. These specially printed letter sheets are designed for microphotography and are screened by the Army censors. Around 0030, we had some bogeys coming over, dropping bombs near the 350th Engineers. One of our P-40 night fighter boys had the bogey spotted but then lost him. Our 90mm guns pounded away into the sky with a deafening rage. We tuned into our short-wave radio for any news.

September 15, 1943 Wednesday

I got some more flying time as Lieutenant Purdy's co-pilot while we practiced bombing runs. New Zealand's rest and relaxation seemed so long ago as we got back into the swing of things. Purdy, Graham and Scott had all been checked out as first pilots.

O.G. Adams was flying in the ship Gopher Gus when he blew a left tire going 70 mph. He veered off the runway and crashed damaging the plane. The plane cracked up immediately before he took off. It was a good shakeup but no one was hurt. Adams went to the hospital that night for observation. Billy G and Timo fixed the aerial so we sat around and enjoyed our new Philco radio.

September 16, 1943 Thursday

I received some letters from home and wrote a few more. Garman and I took a command car to take laundry out and get haircuts at the 44th Seabees. While we were there we inspected a PB2Y four-engine Navy monstrosity which cruises at about 135 mph.

We had a surprise visit at our movie tonight: the first lady, Eleanor Roosevelt, stopped in at COMAIRSOPAC on her tour. She spoke a few words of admiration and respect and wished us all "God speed." She was escorted by a small entourage of brass as she left the stage to a standing ovation. It did a lot to boost the morale of the guys.

In the mail I received from home I was informed that Carl Brink, also of Logansport, is now a German P.O.W.

Chapter 15

September 17, 1943 Friday
Earthquake

Lieutenant Leo Hunt gave me two and a half hours of pilot time today, more transition flying. We flew in formation and were to shoot landings but we had to feather engine number three and come in early. Leo seemed very quiet and calm to me. However, I know some of his crew members have commented, "He's a wild man! When the Japs start firing at us. He starts laughing and screams a rebel yell." All of which seemed to be very unsettling for the rest of his crew.

Word was that Fitz planned to stay his limit at Auckland. Junior was still at Tontouta. Some of the guys, scheduled for return to the States, were Lieutenants Edgar, Burke and possibly Major Riggs. We got home from the movie tonight as the tent floor shook from a small earthquake. Garman and I passed the time by drinking lots of beer we bought at the officers club. A case cost $2.60. The rain was thick and melodious.

September 18, 1943 Saturday
Transition time

Captain John Grace gave me some more flying time as pilot. We were in a Liberator named Jinx. He had me taxiing over the gauntlet strip, which is a fight for an airplane with a wingspan of 110 feet. The B-24 had a length of 67 feet 2 inches and its height was 17 feet 11 inches. I made two landings in the plane and everything went just fine.

Mark Rifkin, a co-pilot, dropped by our tent to let us know he'd been flying with Lieutenant Holmes since Hathaway and his crew had been lost on July 6th.

There was a formal opening of the officers club tonight. I received more letters from home. What a nice distraction.

September 19, 1943 Sunday

Garman and I were listening to new records played over our radio when Mark Rifkin stopped by for a chat. He would be leaving for Auckland the next day. I gave him £3 for flowers and a cable to mother and Patty. Scott, Graham and Lieutenant Vrabel came to our tent in the afternoon for chat and a drink. The guys were giving Rifkin a good briefing on Auckland before his visit, most of which had to do with the local female population.

September 20, 1943 Monday

We were in the midst of the great rainy season down here. I had some beautiful sleep all morning in the driving rain. I got up and answered some letters and finished reading *Pride and Prejudice* by Jane Austen.

Later in the evening, we borrowed a jeep to take in a movie at COMAIRSOPAC, and then drove back to the club for the tail end of some singing. We went to Jutz's galley for fresh eggs and Swift's bacon. Lieutenant Bud Hagerman was thinking about selling us his phonograph pickup. We had Junior negotiating the deal.

September 21, 1943 Tuesday
Tent Life

Another cold and dark night spent writing letters and journal entries. Lieutenants Roark, Wood and Smith literally fell over our stoop. They were lost and headed for our light, apparently the only light burning in the area.

Earlier in the day I had taken my laundry to a French proprietress who offered to pay for my last laundry she lost. Gerry Cass dropped by to ask me to stand by on a search mission with him the next day in the absence of his co-pilot. Later in the evening, Garman and I went to the officers club for a beer. We then had our supper at the mess tent and followed a group of guys headed for the outdoor movie. Since we had been back from Auckland, Clincher hadn't left the ground on any missions. He needed to get back to what he does best, navigating.

September 22, 1943 Wednesday

In addition to catching two rats in our traps the previous night, I supposed the highlight of the day was getting to sit in the cockpit of an F6F Hellcat. It has a much simpler-looking cockpit than the Corsair.

I spent the afternoon catching up on some letter writing. Garman, Lieutenant Don Richardson and I went to the commissary and each bought Meerschaum pipes for $3. Allegedly, they would be worth $7.50 back home. We rode around in a command car surveying the island of Buttons.

September 23, 1943 Thursday

A B-24 from the 307th cracked up on landing yesterday. Fortunately, no one was killed. We stopped on the airfield to look at a C-54 that was on its way home from hauling five generals around.

There didn't seem to be much activity in the squadron these days, with too much drinking and loafing around. I spent some time writing more letters and keeping my diary up to date. The guys and I would be going to another movie at the 13th Air Force that night. Before I left the States a girlfriend had given me a good-luck medal I couldn't find it anywhere.

The island seemed to be overrun with bugs, insects and four-legged critters. Frampton's tent had a cat with a litter of kittens. I supposed they would be put to work before too long. We caught another rat in our tent the previous night. It was off to the club for beers and idle chat. This irritating existence with these unwanted pests was wearing thin.

September 24, 1943 Friday

I spent my morning leisure time making a pipe rack. Major Sansom was back from Auckland to relieve Captain Frampton as C.O. The major said that Fitz would probably leave Auckland on Monday and he was feeling much better. I was told I was to fly co-pilot for Lieutenant Scott tomorrow. We were going to ferry a ship to Guadalcanal.

In the evening I went with Lieutenant Renfro and our crew to get ice cream at the Navy store. The USO unit featured a very smooth tenor, Felix Knight. It was back to our bunks where I finished a letter to a friend of mine, Bob Settles.

September 25, 1943 Saturday
Guadalcanal.

Our plane assigned for the day was number 251, Shamrock. We took off at 0700 with crew chief Donaldson Gorsuch and radioman Leo Wainman. Immediately, we had trouble with the hydraulic system and the radio IFF, (Identification, friend or foe used with radar) which delayed our departure. The radio never did work and we used the emergency approach. We had four F4F Wildcats come up alongside us as we navigated them home. We landed on Cactus to deliver the plane and bring back a group engineer officer, Jimmy Yeates.

While we waited we saw Scootin' Thunder parked in a revetment, all alone. Gorsuch, Wainman and I all stared at our ship. Checking her out to make sure she was still intact. It was time to leave as we collected our cargo and took a last look at Scoot.

We landed back at Buttons at 1555. There was a magazine left in the tent which included the names of the most recent deaths from the squadron; Allan, Roy, Dafoe, Nile, Kinnick, McClelland and Barclay.

It was a depressing end to the day.

September 26, 1943 Sunday

At 0700 Garman and I went to the USS Tryon for breakfast. While there we met Captain Edward Chappell, C.O. of Company E, 103rd of the 45th Infantry Division. He had been wounded on the Munda vendetta and was awarded Silver Stars and a Purple Heart. From there we went to Pier 1 for a sightseeing tour conducted by two captains. We hosted them with wine, whiskey, cigars, cigarettes and magazines.

At 1600 there was a briefing for practice of high altitude bombing of a Jap target, after a triangular course. Since Fitz wasn't back yet, our crew was flying with Lieutenant L.V. Scott. Lieutenant Wicker's crew had been transferred to the 23rd squadron.

Colonel Unruh had been informed by Colonel Burnham that we would go home based on a point system and not by squadrons. This would be an incentive apparently, for individual crews.

Junior had recovered from his illness and was back on Buttons. He came back with several tales about a nurse named Margaret and activity in her tent. So much for his earache.

September 27, 1943 Monday

We were assigned to the ship Geronimo. We took off at 0715 and flew on Major Sansom's left wing, climbing to 21,000 feet. We had eight ships over the target. However, the weather closed in all around so we came in for a landing at 1300 with a 1,500 foot ceiling. It was a rough day of formation flying on oxygen.

Fitz was scheduled to be leaving Auckland today. It would be great to have him back. I hoped he had recovered and was ready to get back to flying. We needed to get our crew working together again as a team, especially with Garman being idle for so very long. He seemed to love the challenge of getting us to our I/P for missions and loves the fact he is always "right on the button."

Chapter 16

September 28, 1943 Tuesday

Today I had to run a few errands with Billy G. First it was to the Frenchwoman's place to drop off laundry. We then had to find a place to get Bill's watch fixed.

About 1030 Fitz landed on Buttons looking fit and eager to return to the business at hand. He brought back several pictures and bottles of rum. The word was spreading that the Navy or Marines were making landings on Kahili or somewhere on Bougainville. We had been assigned ship number 394, formerly called El Bastardo; now it is has been renamed Nitrous Annie.

September 29, 1943 Wednesday

We were scheduled to begin our next stint of combat missions the day after next when we went back to Cactus (Guadalcanal). We had our entire crew back together on a test hop and gunnery mission. While flying in formation, we saw Silver Streak, a stripped B-17 which we caught up to and easily cruised alongside. I checked the speed and we were traveling at 175 mph. At 1530 we came in for a landing.

Good news for Joe Kerwin, he got to go back to the States directly from Auckland. Our new gunner was a young guy named Don Lawson. I also heard that Red Noland is being checked out as an assistant engineer to Gorsuch.

September 30, 1943 Thursday

Bud Hagerman finally decided to sell his record player to us for $75. We had several records we kept playing again and again, mostly Sinatra and some of the big bands; Tommy Dorsey and Glenn Miller. I thought I had converted Al "Kahili" Cohen to a Sinatra fan. It took a great deal of playing his records over and over again to convince our resident funny guy.

We got word that our flight to Guadalcanal had been cancelled until Oct. 2nd. I stayed up to write a letter to my mother. I wanted to ease her mind about some of the missions and raids our crew had had in the past four months. I didn't regret this experience at all. It was a unique education in courage, comradeship, loyalty, responsibility and patriotism. I only hoped there was something more for me to learn and experience. What was the purpose of all this fighting if not for something better? I knew the crew and I was up for the challenge and would see it to its conclusion.

October 1, 1943 Friday

Lieutenant Wicker had to make a water landing off Pallukio Bay. His co-pilot and radio operator were both killed. They were trying to get in some extra transition flying time. I would rather be in action than dying in a practice run. This waiting around was boring and dulled the senses.

October 2, 1943 Saturday
Return to Guadalcanal

I didn't know if this was such a great way to start our second stint but it was almost comical. We loaded our junk onto Nitrous Annie. Gorsuch noticed trouble with the hydraulic brake pressure and the brakes went out completely on our turn onto the runway. The plane crashed across the ditch, tearing off the wingtip against a tree.

We then transferred all our things onto Balls O'Fire but couldn't get cleared because of the status of this ship. The next plane we took was number 213. We finally got to take off at 1115. We were to land at Henderson Field on Cactus and came in for a landing as scheduled. We looked around and noticed the airfield was barren of all B-24s. They had all been sent to Carney Airfield several miles away.

We were given new instructions from the tower at Henderson to take off again, destination Carney Airfield. When we came in for a landing, we spent another 45 minutes in our ship taxiing all over the place looking for a place to park and shut her down. The airfield was swarming with bombers.

The crew finally got to unload their things and we were driven to our Quonset huts which would be our new homes for a while. We had been temporarily assigned to fly The Jolly Roger. She was a good ship and we felt comfortable about our scheduled strike on Kahili the next morning. Lieutenant Adams dropped by our hut tonight and Fitz gave him a bottle of wine.

October 3, 1943 Sunday

The briefing began at 0900 for the next raid on Kahili. A message was received from Colonel Unruh that our mission had been postponed for 24 hours; more than likely due to weather. The Jolly Roger was flown back to Buttons with its original crew so we were without a ship. It felt like a game of musical bombers.

Because of the latest development, our crew had been grounded until Unruh's return so that we could use his ship. The latest news going around on Carney was that there had been a recent raid on Nauru. A whole squadron of Army B-24s got over the target individually, while only two of the 12 Navy B-24s (PB4Y's) found the place. Crack Navy pilots and navigators…Hah!

We spent the afternoon building shelves and cabinets to be able to hang our clothes and hold our radio and record player. The radio reception isn't very good without the aerial or ground.

October 4, 1943 Monday

The rest of our squadron hit their targets on Kahili at about 1330. They were intercepted near Tonolei Harbor taking out four Zeros. Lieutenant Scott came back with an aerial bomb hole through one of his wings. Lieutenant Hunt also had some damage to his ship. Lieutenant Adams turned back at the northern tip of Choiseul with a bad number three engine. He said, just before their landing, the number four engine had the oil pressure drop to 30. The normal cruising pressure is 65 to 80 pounds. They narrowly squeaked by a major incident and all the ships returned home safely.

Harris and I climbed banyan trees to string aerial for our radio so that we would get better reception. During the strike, Fitz had been the tower officer for six hours. Two of the 307th squadrons raced their engines all the way home. While all this was happening the Navy was supposed to be striking in simultaneous effort with their SBDs and TBFs. However, it was cancelled so our boys were caught short with only six P-38s for their fighter escort.

October 5, 1943 Tuesday

There was an electrical storm approaching as a briefing was being held at 2100. Our strike for the next morning would be on the Buka Passage Airdrome. Our crew has been assigned to ship number 786 with Colonel Burnham at the controls. Fitz would be in the co-pilot seat and I was assigned to take pictures with a 12-inch aerial camera. We would be flying in position number two on Major Sansom's right wing.

The 72nd was the number two squadron assigned to the target area, which supposedly contained Mitsu bombers. The 370th Squadron of the 307th Group would be in the number three position. Our alternate target was the Bonis Plantation Airdrome. We were told that 32 fighters would make a sweep over Kahili at 1115, fifteen minutes after we hit Buka. We left the briefing hut into the pouring rain.

Lieutenant Youngheim would make his first combat mission the next day and seemed a bit nervous. It would be our 22nd mission. We knew pretty much what to expect and had to approach it as just another day on the job. Yet, it was never routine and we couldn't get complacent. We needed to expect the unexpected. This had a tendency to keep the adrenalin flowing and the hair on the back of your neck at attention. I completely understood what Youngheim and the rest of his crew are wondering. All of us went to the outdoor theater that night to watch "Arsenic and Old Lace."

October 6, 1943 Wednesday

The raid was cancelled due to the bad weather. Clincher and I went back to our hut and painted ink wings on our leather jackets. Later we went to Koli Field with Lieutenant Lord and Lieutenant Cass to ferry back ship number 266 which we would use on the raid the next day. They flew the plane back while I drove the jeep home to Carney. At 2100 we went back over the briefing for the morning raid.

October 7, 1943 Thursday
Strike on Bougainville

We took off at 0745 in the ninth position. However, Lieutenants Scott and Cass were the number three men in the first and second elements but had to drop out. So we, in ship number 266, a wreck with 40 missions on her, moved up to Major Sansom's left wing. Fitz appeared tense and I thought I would lighten the moment and opened the window of the cockpit and let the rain and wind hit my face and head. I told Fitz, "I bet it will make my hair grow." It got a laugh and he settled down and we were on our way up the slot.

The 307th barreled up Bougainville way, full steam. We climbed to 20,500 feet and found a clear spot west of Kahili near the coastline. Junior gave the "bombs away" at 1110 and we released our frag cluster bombs along the strip. We had heard that the day before, B-25s reported great activity in the same area. We turned for home dodging thunderheads all the way. We landed at 1330 and Fitz and the other first pilots went to their debriefing. He came back and told us the mission was rated unsatisfactory. The only four ships over the target were us, Colonel Burnham, Major Sansom and Lieutenant Lord.

Garman and I took a jeep and drove back to Koli Field to pick up a canteen I had left in the plane. When I got back to the hut I had a letter from home. My friend, Howie Johnson, had just become a father. He had a daughter born August 1st, Susan Gayle.

October 8, 1943 Friday
New Hebrides

Fitz and I rode back to Buttons as passengers. We would be flying back in ship number 155. While we were there, Fitz located some phonograph records at the PX office.

October 9, 1943 Saturday
Guadalcanal

We took off from Buttons at 0800 after loading our supplies from the PX. We needed to build new bomb bay racks and would be bringing these parts with us on our return to Cactus. On the way back we led a P-70 (a night fighter) to Guadalcanal. Our scheduled strike the next day would once again be Kahili. We were assigned plane number 752, Fuzzy Wuzzy, which might become our permanent ship. After dinner, another horseshoe game with Captain Frampton's crew. Garman and I were still the number one team at horseshoes. Doc Schindler and another guy were playing one-man volleyball.

Chapter 17

October 10, 1943 Sunday
Strike on Kahili

We would be flying on Colonel Unruh's left wing. Our takeoff was right at 0855. We flew down the slot and into the target at 1121. Our altitude was 15,000 feet as we dropped our bombs then broke away to the right.

Noland shouted, "Lieutenant we have Zeros at three o'clock! They're out of my range."

Fitz looked up and said, "Bob, look—they're at twelve o'clock." I saw the Zeros racing ahead of us and out of range of our .50-caliber guns.

I said, "Fitz, they're more at one o'clock to me."

Both of us kept our eyes on the two Zeros as they waggled their wings signaling the imminent attack. In unison the Zeros rolled over on their backs and peeled into our formation. Fitz, not taking his eyes off the Zeros, said, "If I get hit get ready to take over."

The pink and yellow tracers came streaming towards our cockpit. I said, "I think they're aiming at me and not you." The Jap pilots knew to go for the third engine, which controlled the hydraulics. The scary part was that the co-pilot was closest to engine three.

The Zeros flew by, missing our ship, and raked Captain Frampton's cockpit. His plane My Baby Bub, slid out of formation then reared into a violent stall and fell away into a spin. I saw three guys bail out. Two of them opened their chutes immediately and were strafed by Zeros and probably killed. One delayed the jump and popped his chute out of the top hatch. It had barely blossomed when the ship crashed into the sea between Bougainville and Choiseul, its nose glowing red hot from the fire within.

The officers lost were Captain Frampton, pilot; Purdy, co-pilot; Lieutenant Farrar, their navigator; and Lieutenant Sheppard, their bombardier. Second Lieutenant Charlie Konkle was on board as a cameraman to earn extra points so he could go home to the States sooner. Fitz and I watched in disgust as the Japs opened fire on these men bailing from their crippled plane. I knew it was war but this really made me angry. I am sure anyone else that saw this felt the same. These guys were easy targets for the Japs. Fitz mumbled, "I hate this war."

Another Zero put a hole through Lieutenant Lord's aileron while another plane from the 307th Group made a crash landing on Munda. The chief cause for the Liberators' trouble was inadequate fighter cover. We only had 16 P-38s with us.

The bombs walked down the Kahili runway perfectly with nine planes over the target. Our tail gunner, John G. Mattson, bagged a Zero. He and Junior Harris saw it hit the water in flames. There was good visibility as we had about eight Corsairs flying at 15,000 feet over us. We met over Bougainville when a P-38 squadron leader called Major Sansom on the way to the target and warned, "Next time to insist that 16 fighters could not cover the force."

All total, we got 280 100-pound bombs smashing into the Kahili runway. On our return flight home there was a lot of chatter. This was just our way of dealing with the horrible crash we had witnessed only minutes before. Eleven men we knew very well were all dead. Twenty four hours ago we had been joking and playing horseshoes with these guys from Frampton's crew.

I don't know what got into Fitz as we approached the airfield at Cactus. For a moment he must have thought he was piloting a fighter as he swooped down and then buzzed the field. We landed at 1324.

When the plane came to a stop I looked over at him and said, "Oscar! What do you think you are doing? What are you thinking? We just survived a strike on Kahili only to have you come in for a landing putting the entire crew in jeopardy by your aerial stunt and buzzing the field?" I know my tone of voice was serious and I got his attention.

Fitz is a great pilot but sometimes his judgments lack maturity. He took what I said to heart and looked like a kid getting scolded. He realized what I said was correct and nothing more was said about the incident.

October 11, 1943 Monday

We were ready for another mission when Major Sansom took our plane and asked Fitz to be his co-pilot on the Kahili raid. Our plane was with the mechanics being repaired so the rest of us had to stay behind. Fitz had had to go on several extra combat missions without the rest of his crew.

All the ships got back from the raid OK. Captain Pierce claimed a Zero. Fitz informed us that one ship that had been bombed the night before was a mass of flames and burned for 36 hours.

We ate dinner in the mess tent then went to the outdoor movie. You had to get there a bit early if you wanted a decent seat. Fitz asked me to save him a place while he showered and said he would meet us there. The feature was some Abbott and Costello movie, and halfway through it was interrupted by an air raid. Everyone scrambled to get out of the way. Benches were tossed; metal railings were bent with dozens of guys trying to get to shelter. There were a few minor injuries for the guys that took their time to get out of the way.

After the realization that there were no Jap bombers nearby and the raid had been a false alarm, the four of us decided to go back to the barracks for some ping-pong and ice cream. We walked into the hut to see Timo standing at attention when we heard Colonel Unruh ask him, "Did you fire your .45 at that steel helmet?"

I wondered "Oh geez, what did the gremlin do now?" Timo's response to the Colonel: "Sir, it was my finger that pulled the trigger."

The four of us tried hard not to laugh out loud. What kind of an answer was that? Everyone in the hut was silent as we looked at Unruh for his reaction. I even think Unruh wanted to laugh, but he stayed true to form and proceeded to lecture Timo for the next five minutes on the dangers of firing an automatic weapon at a steel helmet. I think the gremlin was rattled by the air raid, but got the message loud and clear.

Unruh walked out of the hut passing by us, slightly shaking his head in disbelief. When the door closed behind him Garman looked at Timo and said,

"The air raid was outside, Timo. Did you happen to see some Japs wandering around by our bunks trying to steal our pillows?" He got a good ribbing from all the guys and we laughed at his expression when the Colonel had him at attention. Afterwards, we had ice cream and watched the two Williams play a game of ping-pong. Clincher won.

October 12, 1943 Tuesday

It was the rainy season down here and the heaviest I'd seen yet. It really peppered down, turning the ground to mud-sloshed sinkholes. We spent the day in the barracks working on painting a mural on the wall. There were P-51s, Zeros and P-38s adorning the inside of our hut. We were given the OK to be able to send home Jap souvenirs. Fitz won $20 playing cards.

October 13, 1943 Wednesday

It was still raining as I received more letters from home. Some of the boys got some more paint from the 394th and continued working on the mural. We watched as a new crew came in from Cactus. They would be taking Frampton's crew tent. The pilot was Second Lieutenant Wilson, a bombardier named Lieutenant Tony Kuhn and a navigator named Lieutenant Pandzik. These guys had only four combat missions so far. The raid on Buka had been delayed for 24 hours due to the weather.

October 14, 1943 Thursday

Clincher built a support for our ping-pong table. We made ice cream in the afternoon and played ping-pong. Later we went to the movies to see "The More the Merrier."

October 15, 1943 Friday
Carney Airfield

The squadron took off in the morning for Kahili. Our ship was still out but was supposed to be ready in the afternoon when the new brake metering valves are installed. Apparently, we had been landing with only half our brakes. We got news of the Rabaul strike which knocked out some 200 Jap planes and six ships. Our ships sank a barge near Kahili.

Fitz, Gorsuch, Adams and I test-hopped another ship today. I flew takeoff and landings. Carney air strip was the roughest in the South Pacific, I believed. A dip in the runway swung you to the left on takeoff.

October 16, 1943 Saturday
Strike on Kahili

The briefing for the Kahili strike was at 0515 with the squadron taking off at 0630. Our 24th combat mission saw us over the target at 0930. We flew on Colonel Burnham's left wing. Our takeoff was delayed ten minutes after a fuse and meshing solenoid trouble with our number one and two engines.

We picked up the P-38s and F-40s at 15,000 feet over New Georgia. Leo Hunt's number three engine caught fire and blew a cylinder. He feathered the engine and returned home. Our flight out to the I/P consisted of dodging heavy cumulus clouds all the way there. At 0935 and at 11,500 feet we dropped our bombs on the southern end of Bougainville, and then broke away to the left. We flew in circles for two hours. This was Unruh's first boner on record that I knew of. His navigator obviously couldn't get his bearing. We were off course and sweating out our fuel situation.

Apparently lost, the lead ship had dropped to 800 feet over the Shortland Island and ack-ack started as we were a few miles off the coast. The clouds were all that saved our hides.

The lead ship finally asked for lost plane procedure but Major Sansom and navigator Millikan took over and brought the formation in straight to the Carney airfield. Leo Wainman, our radioman, picked up Cactus homing station about

200 miles out and we came in and landed at 1330. We had logged seven and a half hours of formation flying and were thoroughly exhausted.

October 17, 1943 Sunday
Colonel Unruh honored

At an afternoon dress revue, Colonel Unruh was presented with a Silver Star for work in a strike at Kahili in February. Later in the day, a challenge ping-pong game between Doc Schindler and me. I won the match and would have to take on all challengers. Our briefing for the next day's strike would be at 0615.

October 18, 1943 Monday
Strike on Ballale

This was our 25th combat mission and I had just been promoted to First lieutenant. Our plane was Fuzzy Wuzzy and she was loaded down with six 1,000-pound bombs. This was a very rough runway as Fitz struggled to get her lifted in time to clear the trees at 0734. We were still having trouble with the brake pressure. Fitz had to skid the plane sideways on the Marston mats covering the runway, pulling up just in time to clear the taller trees at the end of the strip. We would be joining squadrons from the 424th, 370th and 307th.

Over the harbor our gas started to siphon out of the number two engine. Gorsuch pumped out some fuel and into the number one engine. We circled over Tulagi and Savo Islands climbing to 10,000 feet. We had to rendezvous with the 307th over Savo. From there, we flew in formation to Choiseul climbing to 18,000 feet to meet up with our P-38 escorts. We then descended to 10,000 feet on course to our target, releasing our bombs at 1036.

Some SBDs and TBFs were hitting Ballale 14 minutes in front of us. Garman took a picture of Kahili off our right wing. We were turning for home when we were jumped by 30 Zeros who pressed a close attack for the next 30 minutes. We had gotten 28 ships over the target with 60 1,000-pound bombs ripping down the middle of the Ballale strip.

Our new waist gunner, Staff Sergeant Lawson, bagged a Zero, while Captain Pierce got a 20mm hunk taken out of the leading edge of the left vertical fin. His tail gunner got a slug in his shoulder and in the seat of his pants. A major who was a flight surgeon happened to be on his ship and treated him.

We flew past Munda and saw the SBDs and TBFs landing. We got back to Carney, landing at 1300. After the debriefing I talked with Fitz; the results of the mission were: we had 28 ships over the target carrying 102 tons of bombs, all of which hit right down the middle of the Ballale strip.

October 19, 1943 Tuesday

Major Sansom's ship was still out of service so he took Fitz and our ship on another Kahili strike. Junior, Clincher and I had to stay home again. When Fitz returned he supplied us with the events and how they unfolded.

The raid had been successful and the ships were turning for home when they were jumped by 20 Zeros. Our nose gunner, Homer "Red" Noland, bagged a Zero, Fuzzy Wuzzy's third. Fitz told us that two P-38s collided when they were shifting position. One of them sheared off the other's wing. He saw one of the fighters crash into the sea while the other was able to land on Vella LaVella. The B-24s overlapped each other in anxiety when the Zeros started pressing their attack. One P-38 went into cloud cover over Vella Lavella and that's when the accident happened. Fitz was dead tired and fell asleep on his cot fully dressed.

Chapter 18

October 20, 1943 Wednesday

The new shower facilities were finished at the edge of the river and right outside of the hut. We played volleyball and ping-pong to pass the time. Later, Junior, Pandzik (Wilson's navigator) and I drove to Henderson Field, special service office. The ping-pong table needed to be painted so we picked up some green paint and a box full of ping-pong balls. Junior got a ticket for speeding from the MP on the way back to camp.

When we got back to Carney we painted the table that was moved inside the Quonset hut. There was a torrential rain storm going on outside so we passed the day by reading, writing letters home, listening to the radio and waiting for the paint to dry.

October 21, 1943 Thursday

More rain! Ten ships of the 23rd squadron arrived including Hagerman and Wicker. Wick is now a Captain.

Colonel Unruh called a meeting before the movie and announced the 5th Bomb Group will function as an independent group and not with the 307th any more. That is good news for us.

In addition, we were told the 72nd would hit Kahili the next day. We would be leading four squadrons who would hit at approximately one-hour intervals. It looked as though the big push for Kahili was underway in earnest.

Our briefing was scheduled for the next morning at 0545. We were expected to be over the target by 0930 with the 23rd hitting at 1025. Recent photo reconnaissance indicated only about two dozen fighters were on Bougainville. However, S-2's Captain Marquart reports replacement at Rabaul and a possible surprise in strength there.

October 22, 1943 Friday
Strike on Kahili

Our briefing was at 0545 with our takeoff at 0655. The 72nd Squadron would be flying with an escort of 24 F6F Hellcat fighters that we picked up over Choiseul. The 23rd Squadron was scheduled to strike an hour later. We passed them on our way home. We also encountered a passel of P-38s zipping by us, traveling like blue blazes.

We didn't get official credit for the mission because we had to turn back with number two engine feathered, cracked rocker box and leaking oil. We need an engine or cylinder change before we fly again. The boys reported back that the target was closed in so they dropped their bombs at 0940 on a dead reckoning course.

Lieutenant Colonel Unruh was promoted to a full Colonel!

We left Fuzzy Wuzzy in the capable hands of the ground crews to see to her immediate needs. Most of us guys went back to the barracks for a long talk that night about sex, religion, love etc. It seemed Junior ran off after the mission and got a SCAT
(Southern Cross air transport) ride to Munda point. He got back about 2100 with Lieutenant Gifford. Who knew what the boy had been up to? It was always interesting to see some of the items Junior had managed to procure on his return.

October 23, 1943 Saturday

Colonel Unruh was still doing roadwork. He obviously liked to stay fit and the exercise kept him in shape. That boy was an inspiration to all of us.

Buzz Youngheim lost an engine supercharger over the target. There was a mix-up over the interphone and some 1,000-pounders tore off the bomb bay doors. Lieutenant Fuller had to lean over the open bomb bay at 18,000 feet and chop off the door that had partially broken off.

That night, I wrote a few paragraphs in my diary on Scootin' Thunder. The guys convinced me to put away the diary and join them in hitting the bottle. Clincher, Fitz and I had a bit to drink and enjoyed the evening rehashing the latest missions. It got a bit somber when Fitz said he had overheard some of the other first pilots talking about him one night. He had returned to his barracks late and some of the pilots were saying things like, "Fitz is a wild kid, he takes too many risks and is going to wind up killing himself and his crew."

Clincher and I could see the distress on his face. I said, "Fitz, they don't know you like we do. You are one of the best damn pilots out here. Don't waste your time worrying about what they think. When you're in that seat at the controls, you are doing what you do best." With that we had another drink and changed the topic to what we all thought and dreamed of nightly, the love of a good woman, a family and what the future would hold for us…if we had a future.

October 24, 1943 Sunday

Word had been spreading that during the Munda raid a Zero had been captured and was over at Henderson Field. Lieutenants Harris, Garman, Pandzik, Kuhn, Eagen and I went over to see it. It wasn't there! Wainman went to church with Fitz. All the rain had caused the river to overflow the banks on both sides. Even the foxholes were now flooded.

It looked as though we were slowly losing our whole squadron; Lieutenant Burke broken leg; Lieutenant Gray and Lieutenant R. Lewis crash nerves; Major Riggs hernia; Lieutenant Edgar health bad; Lieutenant Cass eye trouble; Lieutenant Jess Crume malaria; Lieutenant Jim Moore kidneys; Joe Kerwin, our waist gunner, back to the States; Captain Frampton's crew of 11 men killed in the crash of October 10th over Choiseul.

October 25, 1943 Monday
Test flight

We performed a test flight of "Fuzzy Wuzzy" in the morning after having a cylinder change on the number two engine. Garman was on the first hop with us but then got off after the first landing and went home. Gorsuch checked the sump for filings; it was OK so Fitz, Gorsuch, Wainman, Adams and I flew for another hour. I took off and landed in a slight crosswind.

We got back and were told the 307th had lost a B-24 and its crew at Kahili, over Choiseul. It had stalled out and spun in while in formation through overcast conditions. Another ship also stalled; actually, it slow-rolled over with 8 1,000-pound bombs and they all came back. It was amazing they survived.

At 1800 another briefing was held for the next day's strike on Kahili. A colonel from a fighter squadron gave a talk on cooperation. The main cooperation we were interested in was to make sure the fighters showed up and protected these flying boxcars. We had to stay focused on the strike in front of us and shouldn't have had to worry "if" the fighters were surrounding us.

October 26, 1943 Tuesday
Raid on Kahili

We had a scheduled mission that had the 23rd and 72nd Squadrons working in conjunction with a squadron of PB4Ys from the Navy. Our target, once again, was Kahili as we took off at 0710. We had an escort of 16 P-38s as we climbed to an altitude of 19,000 feet.

A serious problem developed when the Navy planes, flying above us, dropped their 1,000-pound bombs through our formation below. This forced the third and fourth elements of the Air Corps to pull to the left to get out of the way of the bombs. Junior called out "bombs away" at 1030. We managed to get 20 of our planes over the target releasing our bombs and then turned for home.

The ack-ack was close as hell, twice as black and very accurate. It had strung out in pearl chains gradually finding our altitude. The loud booms then the black smoke billowed all around us rocking the planes. Fortunately, no one was hurt. We had 114 1,000-pound bombs hit the target despite the Navy crowding out and overrunning the lead squadron. We brought our plane in for a landing at 1300. Later, it was decided not to use the Navy again.

October 27, 1943 Wednesday

We had the day off and filled it with volleyball before lunch. Junior had just gotten back from Henderson Field with enough ping-pong balls to float a B-24.

I wrote a letter at the request of Buzz Youngheim recommending medals for Lieutenant C.L. Fuller, bombardier, and S/Sgt. C.A. Miller, tail gunner, for chopping off the bomb bay doors after the mishap of the last Kahili raid.

L.V. Scott came into our tent to let us know that we had the Air Medal and Distinguished Flying Cross on the way. The P-38 pilots claimed 1,100 Jap casualties in the surprise strafing at Buka passage that day. Our scheduled briefing for the next day is at 0515. Gorsuch painted another bomb on the side of our plane for our 28th mission.

October 28, 1943 Thursday
Raid on Kara Airdrome

We left Carney Airfield at 0630. Colonel Reddoch would be leading the group of Liberators over the strip, northwest of Kahili. The squadron would be performing column bombing of the Kara Strip.

Our altitude was 19,000 feet when we released our 1,000-pound bombs at 0930. The bombs hit the center of the runway and dispersal areas. The 23rd Squadron walked up the runway leaving a trail of devastation behind them. There was some light but level ack-ack and no Zero interception on this, our 28th mission. We flew in formation home where we ran into a bit of difficulty.

Barclay of the 23rd Squadron cut us out of the traffic pattern, so Fitz had to cut out Pierce of the 72nd. We were given the red light by the tower and came in for a landing with our left brake not working. We looped off the center runway and stopped against a pile of coral. All things considered, this was an excellent mission with 19 planes over the target, releasing 112 1,000-pound bombs.

Fuzzy Wuzzy was taken to the 29th Service Group for "de-sabotaging." Her hydraulic line was full of iron filings that had to be flushed. They would also do a controls check before letting us go up with her again. The mess had been feeding us Vienna sausage and spam for a week now. Where was the Navy when you needed them? Maybe we would have Junior look into getting us something different.

October 30, 1943 Saturday

The squadron is on a raid to Kara again. Our ship is out of service so we were grounded. Fitz flew with Cass and his crew while the rest of us stayed on the ground. The weather was very hot and humid so I took my cot out to the middle of the Tenaru Malimbire river bank to get some sun. The boys ganged up on shore and stoned me!

I spent the rest of the afternoon writing some letters home and repainting some of my flight jacket.

October 31, 1943 Sunday
Halloween

Harris and I stole a jeep and hunted out a movie. When we returned we were challenged by a Negro guard when we stumbled onto Koli Field in the dark. We turned and headed back to Carney.

November 1, 1943 Monday
Marines on Bougainville

That morning it was reported that Marine forces had landed on Bougainville Island at 0600. There were four aircraft carriers and some ack-ack ships. Fitz had to fly with Cass' crew while crew number 100 stayed home again. The three squadrons of B-24s had a poor run on Kara Field, according to Fitz when he returned.

We checked on Fuzzy Wuzzy in the afternoon and the 29th Service Group OK'd her for flying the next day. I hated to be paranoid about this ship but, it concerned me because of all the minor things that kept happening. It seemed that we had been very lucky and I guessed I was worrying when the luck will change. Garman, Harris and I went to a Jap lecture that night.

November 2, 1943 Tuesday
Alert.

We were up at 0415 for a briefing alert. We would be on a two-hour standby all day to hit the shipping area following a naval engagement at Empress Augusta Bay. The 5th Group Project Squadron snooper ship had located a Jap task force at 2100 the day before.

Apparently, eight DDs (destroyers) and four CAs (heavy cruisers) were spotted by our snoopers as they followed them until 0100 making six passes but hitting nothing.

Our force of 12 DDs and four CLs (light cruisers) of Cleveland Class engaged them at 0300. However, there was no further report or engagement and we did not have to take off.

In addition to this news, we were told of the first men of our squadron that would be going home about November 20th. The four navigators Lieutenant Hamshaw, Millikan, Lieutenant Les Mann and Melvin Tiemann (Timo), would be the first lucky guys to make it out of here. The replacements were supposed to be at the rate of four crews every three weeks. The crews, according to position on airplane, are selected from all air forces here. Hence, four pilots, co-pilots, navigators, bombardiers, engineers, etc. Whoever has the greatest number of points would leave regardless of crews as units.

Fitz had seemed very depressed the past few days. Since we had to give Scootin' Thunder to the 31st Squadron, he had been wondering when "our time" will come. I talked to him and told him it was "his skill" and not the plane that had seen all of us through these combat missions. At times he had lost confidence in himself. I knew this was a maturing process for him and he needed to realize and understand the crew and I had confidence in him. I spoke to him like a big brother then gave him a shove and said let's go to the officer's club and get a drink.

Chapter 19

November 3, 1943 Wednesday
Munda, New Georgia

We had a briefing at 0415. Our instructions were to fly to Munda point, refuel and then go on to Kavieng. We were flying Fuzzy Wuzzy loaded with six 1,000-pound bombs. The squadron took off and had a pleasant enough flight on its way to Munda. However, things changed rapidly as we descended to the coral runway that was still under construction.

The weather was miserable as we came in for a landing at 60 miles per hour. We touched down and noticed immediately that our brakes started to slip near the end of the runway. Fitz jammed on his brakes then said to me, "Try your brakes." I pushed the brakes as far as they would go and I answered back, "Nothing." We could both see the large land-moving equipment left by the Seabees at the end of the runway. It was Fitz's quick thinking and cleverness that took over, proving his skill once again. He immediately shut down engines one, two and three and gave full throttle to engine number four. The momentum of our speed and engine number four pulled us hard to the left where our plane proceeded to climb to the top of a 20-foot knob hill, which we plowed into, holding the nose high. We slipped up the hill, spun around and stopped perched on the top. The left wheel was caught in a hole which kept us from any further movement. The props of the plane tore to shreds a tent that had been occupied by some of the Seabees. They saw us coming and ran for their lives.

It was a close shave with those fused bombs aboard. Fitz shut down the engine and we sat for a moment to catch our breath. I said, "Nice landing." We were looking down on the runway as we saw ground crews running towards us. Everyone wanted to know how in the hell we got a B-24 on top of that knot. Our crew felt lucky to have made the landing without crashing and setting off the bombs on board. However, we knew that we would miss the scheduled raid and the squadron would have to proceed without us. On one hand, the crew was relieved to be safely on the ground, and yet angry that the faulty brakes kept us out of an important strike on the shipping forces at Kavieng.

The Seabees bulldozed the road and pulled Fuzzy Wuzzy off the hill and off to a remote area clear of the runway. There were no extra planes so we had to stay grounded while the rest of the 72nd and the 23rd Squadrons took off at 0930 to hit the shipping northeast of Kavieng, on New Ireland. Colonel Unruh was out front leading the way. The runway was congested with all the Liberators getting in line and the rain turned the coral strip to mud and slush. The prop wash from these bombers kept everyone on the ground at a distance.

We spent the rest of the day out of the rain but were on standby waiting for the Squadrons return.

When we got word the ships were returning all available men were at the airstrip watching the planes come in for a landing. We looked up to see several of the planes passing overhead and heading for an alternate landing field. The reason soon became apparent. Colonel Unruh buzzed the strip in the Pretty Prairie Special and shot off some flares. This was a signal to everyone on the ground that a badly damaged plane was coming in for an emergency landing.

Ambulances, jeeps and ground crews were at the ready when we saw the ship: Huggermugger, approaching and descending with one engine feathered and smoke pouring from another. She hit the runway without rudder control then we heard the nose wheel collapse. All able bodies sprang into action. The colonel circled the field and came down and landed on the second approach.

Huggermugger, Captain O.G. Adams' plane had landed with part of her tail gone, gun turrets riddled with bullet holes and the plane, looking like a sieve from all the holes shot in her. The tail gunner, Ed Watkins, was bleeding profusely with 7.7 mm shells sticking out of him. Harris and I very carefully placed Watkins into a waiting ambulance. The plane had the instruments, aileron cable and hydraulic system shot out. The waist gunner, Phillips, was shot in the stomach.

Captain Adams said he had had no manual control of the aileron and his number three engine went out with a 7.7 mm hole through all three blades so he switched to the AFCE control for rudder and oil and landed that way, operating the elevator manually. The crew had managed to crank the wheels and flaps down by hand but when the nose wheel collapsed she nosed over and skidded slowly to a stop on the rain-soaked coral runway.

Red hydraulic fluid and oil looked like blood and mud in puddles under the wounded ship. The tail gunner's left arm and leg were broken and he was given two quarts of blood plasma. It was Colonel Unruh and the Pretty Prairie Special that had waved the rest of the squadron home and stayed with Huggermugger, shepherding her down to the field below. Unruh was calm and handled the emergency with great aplomb. The colonel remained an enigma to most of us as he did what was needed at the time of this emergency and never diverted attention to himself. After checking on Adams and his crew and their condition he left to file his report, staying clear of the reporters on the scene.

There was a crowd of us guys checking out Adams' ship. The left rudder had a chunk one-foot square hacked out by a 20 mm shell. All the guns on the plane were tossed out except the 30-mm gun in the nose. The plan of attack had been to have five planes in a vee pattern but Adams had turned out to be the only ship in the 2nd vee of the 72nd squadron. Scott's plane had wandered out of formation and a dozen Zeros jumped Adams. The plane was a mess and so were the nerves of some of the crew. They kept their jitters together and welcomed the assistance of all the airmen on the ground. Every available man on the ground reacted with care and concern for his injured comrades.

The gunners and bombardier were credited with five certain Zero kills. Later, Adams was interviewed by some Marine and AP reporters for a glamorous yarn for the hometown newspapers.

Wilson's crew had to make a water landing north of Bougainville where he, his co-pilot Eagan and four other crew members were lost. Pandzik, Tony Kuhn, an engineer and a radio operator made it out in life rafts and were later picked up. Their plane had been hit by ack-ack, killing the number one and two engines. The feathering knobs had been shot out making it impossible to feather the props. Renfro was credited with two Zeros.

The talk lasted late into the evening where we slept under brand-new white USN blankets on brand-new cots. This was far different and much more comfortable than our home on Carney. I stayed awake wondering if we could have made a difference if our plane hadn't lost her brakes. I guessed some things were out of our control and we would never know. Garman had said, "It wasn't meant for us to go on that mission," and to stop thinking about it.

November 4, 1943 Thursday
Search mission

The 72nd planes took off from Munda point at 0800 to search for Wilson's crew. The four survivors were spotted in two life rafts at 0932. The navigator, Lieutenant Millikan, had made a dead-reckoning course to the last known position of the crash. Major Sansom's plane left while four other Liberators circled the stranded crew members. Harris was riding on Sansom's plane and dropped smoke and slick bombs before they turned for home.

A radio message was sent giving the location southeast of the Kilinailau Islands where Captain Classen had made a forced landing several months ago. The Navy dispatched a Dumbo PBY to rescue these four men. However, they were delayed and the B-24s circled for four hours over the rafts. The PBY finally arrived and landed with fighter cover provided by several P-40s. The stranded men were taken aboard the Navy rescue plane and returned to Rendova Point. The P-40s strafed the now empty life rafts and escorted the PBY home.

Fitz flew to Munda with Lieutenant Kozlowski to take parts for the service crew so that they could repair Fuzzy Wuzzy. Garman and I flew back to Cactus with Bud Hagerman. We buzzed the Segi landing strip on the way home landing back at Carney hoping to regroup with our crew.

November 5, 1943 Friday

The reports back from yesterdays search mission confirmed that navigator Pandzik, bombardier Kuhn and an engineer and radio operator were the only survivors of Wilson's crash. The Dumbo had taken these men to Rendova Island, then Munda. Once they arrived on Munda a DC-3 transported them to Henderson Field on Guadalcanal, then to the 20th Station Hospital.

Pandzik had shrapnel in one of his legs and a badly lacerated scalp which Tony Kuhn had put in place and tied a T-shirt around to help stabilize. The survivors of that crash said they yelled and screamed for joy when they spotted our B-24s on the search. One of their enlisted men is in very bad shape.

Later that day, Fitz, Lieutenant Robison and I went to visit the guys in the hospital. I had Pandzik's wallet with $134 in it. I knew we could get further details when we talked to Tony and Pandzik. They indicated the plane became disabled by all the ack-ack.

Colonel Unruh spoke to the 72nd, 23rd and 5th Bomb Group about all the group project squadrons in the theatre area. He spent a good deal of time going over the Kavieng shipping strike and the things they had learned from the same. We were also told that the next day our mission would be to hit the Bonis Plantation on the southern side of the Buka Passage.

Some photographer took pictures of all the 72nd crews by their airplanes. We already had had our picture taken in front of Scootin' Thunder a while back. Since we didn't have a plane here, we posed in front of Tim-ber, the Major's ship. It wasn't the same. All of us on our crew knew that Scootin' Thunder was our plane.

November 6, 1943 Saturday
Raid on Bonis Airdrome

The briefing began at 0630 with our instructions to take off at 0900. We were assigned ship number 828 and would be leading the second element. Our ships were all armed with 6 1,000-pound bombs.

The 72nd would be following in the trail of the 23rd Squadron. We were to rendezvous with the 23rd over the Manning Strait. Our course was due north through the front extending to 30,000 feet on a 6 degree paralleling Kieta, Buka and Bonis. At 1203 Junior exclaimed, "Bombs away," and our bombs dropped hitting the center of the runway. Our altitude was 18,000 feet.

We were all in a hurry to leave as Garman shouted, "Let's get the hell out of here." We noticed that there were no Zero interceptions but they were fairly accurate with their ack-ack. On our way home we noticed a P-38 grandstanding during the bomb run. The fighter was at about 26,000 feet making a large J-shaped vapor trail. He was probably taking a picture of the scene below.

Our nose turret went out; however, on the way up we noticed many CLs (light cruisers) and DDs (destroyers) on their way to reinforce the Bougainville landing.

We logged seven hours of flight time as we came in for a landing at 1530. I had a miserable head cold which nearly popped my ears at the altitude today and also on the descent. We got back to the barracks to read some more letters from home. All of us were tired but decided to go to the officers club for a beer. It was a successful mission with 17 planes over the target dropping 102 1,000-pound bombs.

November 7, 1943 Sunday

It was my 23rd birthday but I didn't mention it to any of the guys. It seemed like if they found out, they delighted on catching you when you were sleeping and proceeded to beat you…just for fun. I remember how they got Clincher on his 26th birthday. I still had a bad cold. Some of the guys got a jeep and went on a sight-seeing trip to Cape Esperance. I heard we would have another mission on Bonis the next day using 100-pound demos.

November 8, 1943 Monday

The briefing was held at 0700 in the 5th Bombardment Group Briefing Assembly Quonset hut. Our I/P would be the Bonis Airdrome with other large surface vessels near Bonis as our secondary targets. Some CAs (heavy cruisers) were sighted nearby and would become additional targets. With our ship, Fuzzy Wuzzy, out of commission, we were assigned plane number 214, Mary Lou II.

All the Liberators were armed with 40 100-pound demo bombs. We took off at 0822 and had almost closed into position leading the third element when our hydraulic line to those infernal brakes started spurting fluid that covered the co-pilot's floor. I tried to feather the number three engine but had no luck. The hydraulic fluid had eaten through the wires creating a short circuit that couldn't be fixed. Fitz turned the plane back to Carney with the fluid going fast and landed despite the red-light condition on the field. He took Mary Lou right over a B-24 parked in a takeoff position. It was a good thing that the brakes worked OK.

The crew felt cheated again by having to deal with another plane that had hidden troubles. We missed this mission and returned to the barracks with another splotch of inferior luck on our chart.

Fitz, Garman and I took a jeep over to the 20th Station Hospital to see Kuhn and Pandzik, who were coming along well. We stayed there and had lunch in the hospital mess: chicken soup and watermelon. We saw a couple of other guys from another crew, Lieutenant Grace and Lieutenant Byrne, who were also in the hospital with injuries.

When we got back to the barracks some cavalry man stopped by to show us some knife sets he had made from a Jap bayonet and a Jap Zero prop. He will bring me one in two days for a quart of whiskey. Fitz also got one. Clincher traded his whiskey for two Jap ashtrays.

The squadron returned from Treasury because of the bad weather. However, there were eight planes who managed to get over Kara Airfield and unload their bombs. Some of the others; Youngheim, Lord, Colonel Reddoch, Hunt, Scott and Lieutenant Osborne landed at Russell's in overcast conditions. It had been raining very hard most of the day and night.

November 9, 1943 Tuesday

We received word that our crew, Hunt's and Cass' would be transferred to the 394th Squadron for some unknown reason. Tiemann had been scheduled to go back to the States but had his name taken off the list due to Wilson's crew being lost. We would have the gremlin around for a while longer. News was that we would be going to Munda the next day.

November 10, 1943 Wednesday
Munda, New Georgia

Our briefing took place at 1000. This was going to be a large scale raid on the Rabaul harbor as part of a coordinated attack. All squadrons were represented; the 23rd, 72nd of the 5th Group and the 424th and 372nd of the 307th Group.

Several SBDs and TBFs were to hit first from five carriers. The Saratoga and the Princeton were in one task force, with the Bunker Hill, Essex and Independence in the second.

Our instructions were to fly in a diamond formation, one squadron to a target. We would bomb at 70-foot intervals.

Colonel Unruh proceeded to tell us to be on the alert at Carteret and Green Island for float-type planes. We would cross to New Ireland on a southeast heading to our I/P of Walton Island. He went on to say that there had been heavy ack-ack around Simpson Harbor and Blanche Bay. The Liberators would strike at 0945 after the Navy's low altitude bombing. The P-38s would be at 27,000 feet after bombs away.

Our plane, Mary Lou, took off from Carney at 1235 and we noticed a problem almost immediately. Gorsuch told us an oil sump valve had not been safetied on the number one engine and fire and smoke trailed us around the field. We had lost two thirds of the oil in the number one engine as I feathered it and started it again for the landing. We landed with the load of six 1,000-bombs back on Carney.

At 1330 the plane was ready for takeoff and we made it to Munda, landing at 1450. We ate at "Mandy's Mansion" then attended a briefing by Colonel Pritchard. We slept at the Quonset hut of the "Red Raiders," a Navy outfit, finally getting some much needed sleep.

November 11, 1943 Thursday
Raid on Rabaul Shipping

At 0300 we were up for breakfast and then went to our assigned ship, number 828. The 72nd Squadron took off second to fly in the number three position. The 23rd Squadron led the way with the 424th in the number two position and the 372nd in the number four position.

It was 0550 as we took off to rendezvous with the groups at Cape Alexander on Choiseul. We were on course at 0737 to the Kilinailau Island. At 0830 we were crossing over Holanga and at 0917 we were coming across New Ireland noticing cumulus clouds stalking over the target area with good visibility around them. The clouds looked to be 1,000 feet above the water. Every squadron took their target. Our bombs away were at 0937 and we were lost in the clouds, therefore uncertain of our hits.

Colonel Unruh led the 23rd, over the radio, to lower its altitude to bomb another ship. The bombs fell in a very close bracket but the ship sailed out of the spray. The 307th also had indifferent success, proving the dubious worth of high altitude bombing on shipping.

We were headed for home and could see the P-38s above a short way from the target when a lone Zero raced by the entire four squadrons on our starboard side. He tore in front and above the formation and barreled down the alley among us. Many of our guns cut loose and, almost as if the Jap had one hand on his chute, he popped out of his smoking Zero as it crumbled and dived into the drink in brilliant orange flames. The pilot of the Zero had popped his chute right off our right wing as the gunners from several ships opened up on him. What was he thinking? I guess our guys had not forgotten what happened to Frampton's crew that parachuted from a B-24 engulfed in flames.

The Zero was shot down at 1018 and we managed to get 114 1,000-pound bombs on target with an escort of 24 P-38s. We flew through scattered thundershowers landing with 350 gallons of gas back on Munda at 1255.

Colonel Unruh's gunners also got a Zero. Every gunner in the squadron was claiming that Bushido Butch. One ship in the 307th flown by Lieutenant Jelle was lost in a water landing. A co-pilot was killed by a Zero burst and six of his crew bailed out over a friendly convoy. One man was lost.

We landed at Munda and refueled for a takeoff at 1415 on our way back to Guadalcanal, landing at 1545. It was a very hard day. We made it back to the barracks to fall asleep fully dressed on our cots.

Chapter 20

November 12, 1943 Friday
Day of rest

We had a strike scheduled on Bonis for Saturday. Ice cream was served at 1500 with Colonels Unruh, Burnham and Reddoch and Major Sansom in attendance at the get-together.

November 13, 1943 Saturday
Raid Bonis Airdrome

I was flying as pilot as we took off from Carney at 0805. Colonel Reddoch would lead the 72nd Squadron and our plane would be leading the third element. The 23rd Squadron would take off 15 minutes after us and meet us at an altitude of 14,400 feet. When we got over the target we came in at 200-foot intervals. Our bombs were released at 1126, hitting either side of the runway axis of attack.

We didn't encounter any fighter interception but the hail of ack-ack was the heaviest we had yet seen. It started one and a half minutes before we were over the target. Our ship got bounced around a lot but no one was hurt. At times the ack-ack was so close it sounded like a sledgehammer hitting a tin roof.

We headed for home and were on the lookout for any lost aircraft and crew. This mission was rated good as we managed to get 96 1,000-pound bombs stomping down the runway below. It was raining pretty hard as we dodged some scattered thunderheads on the way home, landing at 1440 on Carney.

November 14, 1943 Sunday

We were told to load our ship to go back to Buttons. However, the 31st Squadron did not arrive to replace us so we had to unload and go back to our barracks, awaiting another strike. This delay meant that we would have to go on the next mission in place of the 31st. Several guys were understandably upset and cursed the 31st crews.

November 15, 1943 Monday
Raid Buka Airdrome

Our 32nd combat mission began as we took off at 0938 loaded with 500-pound bombs. The boys from the 72nd would be flying the number two position as we were ordered to come in over the target at 150-foot intervals. Our altitude was 20,000 feet as we let loose our ordnance at 1236.

The ack-ack was heavy as our bombs bracketed the runway with several of the bombs hitting the runway. We got 19 airplanes over the target with 216 500-pound bombs and six 1,000-pound bombs landing on Buka. The weather was generally good and this mission was rated excellent.

On our return, we fanned out southeast of southern Bougainville searching for any lost crew of the 307th. We were warned that the Japs were rumored to have a captured B-24 in flyable condition and to be on the look out for an apparently straggling ship. However, we saw no sign of him.

Fitz brought us back to Carney, touching down at 1450. As we had left for the mission that morning the 31st Squadron was just landing on Carney. This mission should have been theirs.

November 16, 1943 Tuesday
New Hebrides, Buttons

Take off at 0740 and we landed on Buttons, (Espiritu Santo) at 1120. We parked the plane and headed for our messy tent and mail call.

November 17, 1943 Wednesday

Fitz left for Auckland, New Zealand, today. The rest of us were crowded out by high-ranking officials on their way to civilization. We packed to get ready to leave the next day. The thoughts of escaping the fighting for awhile and in such a beautiful place as Auckland made the delay more palatable.

November 18, 1943 Thursday
Auckland, New Zealand

At 0320 we took off for Auckland in a C-47 named Phyllis. We stopped in Tontouta, New Caledonia, to refuel and were back in the air at 0710. We landed in New Zealand at 1435 and all of us were billeted at Kia Ora. We all drove into town to the Waverly Hotel with plans for some dates.

November 19, 1943 Friday

I slept late in spite of my 0830 physical. We had breakfast with Major Sansom and Colonel Councill at Kia Ora. The physical was OK except for very poor depth perception so I'll have to recheck later. Clincher, Harris and I played croquet at Kia Ora.

November 20, 1943 Saturday

Up at 1015 and had breakfast of steak and eggs at 1100. I played tennis with Scott and Fitz at Mrs. Kerridge's court. Later we went shopping in Queen Street and got some Maori god Made of Totara wood.

November 21, 1943 Sunday

I got up late and went to the Waverly for wine cocktails. We got a car and met a Captain who was with Harris on the hospital boat. We met several girls, had dinner and returned home at 0230. Garman and I came had a late night snack of fried steaks in the kitchen and drank very cold milk. It was an exceptional feast.

November 22, 1943 Monday

Woke up at 0930, had some breakfast and played a round of golf. I had parked the car at the speedway on Karangahape Road and when I got back it wouldn't start. We started to walk home and a taxi picked us up and later helped pull the car to get it started. We paid the driver 15 shillings.

November 23, 1943 Tuesday
Rotorua, New Zealand

Youngheim and his crew arrived and were off in Junior's Morris at 1145. We were on Hamilton at 1415 and took off at 1530 arriving at 1730. There were some Red Cross gals from Seattle, Washington, that had gotten us rooms at the Lake House. We danced at Tama (a Maori meeting hall).

November 24, 1943 Wednesday

We went shopping and had lunch at the Lake House. The Red Cross had arranged for us to go on a deer hunt tomorrow at 0300. It was safe to say the deer had nothing to fear from me.

November 25, 1943 Thursday

Garman and I were awake at 0330 to go on the deer hunt. We only found tracks of a deer. We decided to go to the Rotorua Course with Harris for a round of golf. When we returned, they had a Thanksgiving dinner for 30 Americans at the Lake House. We sang the Air Corps song and danced at the Maori Hall. We caught a bus and then walked the girls home.

Junior didn't get home until 0500. I was sure we would hear all about it the next day. We arranged to stay an extra day and saw Mike Lord's picture in the paper with his bride.

November 26, 1943 Friday

Garman and I played a game of tennis on grass courts. We had lunch back at the hotel. When we got back to our room Harris and Lieutenant O'Brien were having their fortunes told by some very large female cook who worked at the hotel. Garman thought it would be fun so he had his fortune told as well. I passed on the idea.

November 27, 1943 Saturday

Clincher, Harris and I got breakfast and then headed back to Auckland. Junior was going to drive us back in his Morris but we soon discovered the gasoline had been stolen out of the tank. Earlier he had been driving 50 miles per hour in this kiddie car when the rods burnt out and we were stalled five miles north of Huntley. Harris called the army post for help as Garman and I hitched a ride to Huntley. We made it to the train at 1600.

November 28, 1943 Sunday

In the afternoon I had a great time playing golf with Sherer, Whitten and Barney. Junior Harris got his car fixed and was driving all over the place. Clincher and I did a bit of shopping to take some things back with us on our return to Buttons. I made sure I had plenty of cigars and pipe tobacco. I can't afford the prices Junior charges.

It was our last evening out before returning to the fight. We had a wonderful dinner and walked around the city, getting home at 0300. We packed our things until 0445 to be ready in time for our flight the next morning. It was a shame to leave this beautiful scenery and weather to go back to the humidity and squalor of Guadalcanal.

November 29, 1943 Monday
Tontouta, New Caledonia

We got back on the C-47 and left beautiful New Zealand at 0900. We stayed the night in New Caledonia. Junior hunted down some nurse and we didn't see him until the early morning. He seemed to be very busy with the ladies on our short stay in New Zealand.

November 30, 1943 Tuesday

The troop C-47 named Phyllis took off at 0530-destination Buttons. I slept all the way there. We landed in heavy rain and there were no lights on our car so we had to convoy by jeep back to our tents. There were some mail and packages from home waiting for me. Unfortunately, we quickly adjusted to being back in the tents. Auckland and its vibrant colors were fading rapidly to the dull drab green of our musty tent city.

Chapter 21

December 1, 1943 Wednesday

I got our radio back from Bucky Stafford. We spent the dreary day listening to some records that I received from home. I had Fitz listen to some classical music as a change of pace from the country music he liked.

December 2, 1943 Thursday

The rain cancelled the 394th flight for that day. There was heavy overcast. I spent the day writing letters and reading. Garman and I went to the Navy store where I got a pipe. I also got one for Gorsuch. After dinner we went to the movie; however, it was bad and the rain was unbearable so we went back to the tent. The steady pounding of the rain has a hypnotic effect and was a pleasant backdrop to the book I was reading.

December 3, 1943 Friday

I got a letter from Wayne Daniel who is overseas with a New York APO 520 (a mail center for letters going overseas). I was third on the co-pilot list to go home and number one on the November 15th list with 9.01 points.

We flew with the 394th, leading the element. However, they were too slow so we scissored to keep our air speed. Another ship took our place so we scared him and ourselves with a bit of tight formation. Fitz had me land the plane. Everything went just fine.

December 4, 1943 Saturday

The latest news was that Grace, Graham, Lieutenant Sanchagrin and Lieutenant Darneal were to go home soon. The 394th Squadron was being sent back to Cactus on December 7th.

Mark Rifkin was back from Guadalcanal on his way to New Zealand. He stopped by to tell us he has 39 strikes and 9.5 points. More rain all day.

December 5, 1943 Sunday

We found out that Captain Andrew Hughes and his crew of the 31st had been shot down over Buka. Seven men had bailed out over the airdrome. Apparently, their plane—Little Chum—went over the target on three engines and was nailed by some ack-ack. Navy PB2Ys would be sent out to search for them. It had been raining five to six times a day.

December 6, 1943 Monday

We packed and loaded our plane. I got some more records from home. It was still raining very hard.

December 7, 1943 Tuesday
Guadalcanal

Gorsuch got us up at 0330 to eat and finish packing. We started the engines at 0500 and waited in line until we were ready to take off at 0530. It was really cold in the pre-dawn morning so we wore our jackets to keep warm. The boys in our crew wore their hats with the earmuffs. The lads seldom complained about the cold. Discomfort was just part of being in the back end of a Liberator; it went along with the job.

We climbed to 11,000 feet to top the thunder clouds. We were the fifth ship to take off and the first to land at the Koli strip in a rainstorm. We got to the barracks that were designated for the 394th and got settled in by wiring the radio and the phonograph. Leo Hunt got a late start leaving Buttons at 1000 and arrived on Cactus about 1400.

December 8, 1943 Wednesday

There was heavy rain all night and at about 0300 a tree limb hit the roof jarring everyone awake including Timo the gremlin. We thought we were under attack and several of us ran for the door. When we got outside we could see the tree uprooted and a large limb resting on our Quonset hut.

Later in the afternoon we had a meeting in S-2 for the 394th orientation by Colonels Burnbaum and Reddoch and Captain Marquardt. We went back to the barracks and spent the evening cleaning our pistols.

December 9, 1943 Thursday

Buzz Youngheim was here on a ferry mission. His ship had gotten stuck when the edge of the taxi area caved in. There was a hurricane north of here that is preventing any strikes. Colonel Unruh came around to see about making some more ice cream. He offered to get the milk.

Chapter 22

December 10, 1943 Friday

Lieutenant Wolfe of the 31st said that some ack-ack shells hit Captain Andrew Hughes that day over Buka. They were flying a ship called Little Chum. The shells hit between the number two engine and the fuselage, sending the ship into a dive eight men bailed out. Then the ship leveled off and slid along the water as it crashed and broke apart. All aboard were lost.

The sunshine broke through and gave us some time on the beach for a little swimming. All the guys made it down to the shore behaving as if they had never seen the sun before. How quickly they forget.

December 11, 1943 Saturday
Raid on Sirogei Village

We were up at 0700 to make our 0900 briefing for the mission. The Sirogei supply area was five miles south of Bonis and we would be leading the second element of this bastard squadron. Several planes from all the squadrons were either in for repair, crashed or cannibalized for parts.

Our plane was armed with 20 100-pound demos as we took off at 1050. We had climbed to 19,200 feet when our tail gunner, John Mattson, told us there was an oxygen leak in the tail turret.

We sighted two U.S. convoys, one of five ships and the other of 18, steaming south at 10 knots. They were well protected by CLs (light cruisers), DDs (destroyers) and corvettes. We broke away to the right and back on a northern direct route. The axis of attack was 27 degrees true with a target 700 feet wide.

At 1416 we were over the target as Junior exclaimed, "Bombs away." The ack-ack was of medium intensity and low to the ground. We had no interception. The 31st Squadron released 1,626 20-pound frag cluster bombs that pummeled the village below. We followed suit, bringing the 72nd Squadron over the target unleashing 275 100-pound bombs. We were able to get 23 of our planes over the target with an escort of only four P-38s flying cover for us.

We landed at 1710 completing our 33rd combat mission with 1,000 gallons of gas still on board.

Several of the lads got drunk and chucked stones at the barracks all night.

December 12, 1943 Sunday

We had fresh eggs for breakfast—what a treat. The commanding officer called in the rumpus-raisers of last night for reprisals. Fitz drove to Koli to have dinner with Bucky Stafford. When he returned he told me they had had a good long talk about their past, present and future. Jack "Bucky" Stafford was a first pilot and experienced a water landing of his plane on August 25th in which he broke his ankle. His radio operator, Lieutenant Albert Feller, was lost in this crash. Stafford and Fitz were good friends and the last two men of their cadet class. Bucky also looked after Fitz after his nasal surgery in Auckland.

December 13, 1943 Monday
Raid on Wong Tu

Our briefing began at 0830 with the orders given for the day's raid. We would be flying over the Buka passage. Our plane was armed with 12 500-pound demo bombs as we took off at 1040. Major Smith, a bomber command flight surgeon, rode in our ship.

We had 22 planes coming in over the target at 18,500 feet. At 1336 the familiar exclamation came from Junior Harris: "Bombs away." The CO, Major Zinn, had his bomb bay doors jam on an empty .50-caliber cartridge. Although we did not have any fighter cover on this mission we managed to drop 264 500-pound bombs with the ack-ack being very light. We came in for a landing at 1630.

December 14, 1943 Tuesday

It was an uneventful day as we made ice cream in the afternoon and sat through the first reel of the Ice Capades in the evening. The first reel was more than I could endure. However, we had to stick around for the briefing that was scheduled after the movie.

We were briefed for the strike the next day on Sohana. Our crew, number 100, would be flying in the number two position in the first element. We would be making individual runs on the ack-ack positions to see if we could knock some of them out. According to the day's report, the 307th Group unloaded 165 500-pound bombs on that place so this should be a wash-up job. We would use 500-pound bombs to finish them off.

December 15, 1943 Wednesday
Raid Sohana Island A/A Position

Everyone was awake at 0500 and getting ready for our next strike. We took off at 0709 and took the northern route up the Solomon Islands. Our altitude over the target was 19,500 feet. We could see New Britain and New Ireland plainly 175 miles away.

At 1003 we set free our payload and turned for home. A ship from the 31st Squadron strayed from the element and we almost collided. There were ships all over the sky. We broke off from the squadron and flew over Russell's on the way home landing at 1305. The mission was rated good with 246 500-pound bombs penetrating the target below. We returned with less than half our supply of fuel.

December 16, 1943 Thursday

We had the day off. However, Noland, Gorsuch and Fitz drove out to the airfield to work on our plane. Later in the evening we all went to the outdoor movie getting soaking wet sitting through a thunderstorm to see "Great Man's Lady."

December 17, 1943 Friday

American troops had seized the coastal section of south New Britain with land, sea and air surprise attacks as of Wednesday. We made out our pay vouchers and were briefed for a Rabaul mission with a scheduled take off the next day at 0715. We also willed all our belongings to the fellows not going on the Rabaul mission tomorrow.

December 18, 1943 Saturday
Raid Kahili, Target I

We were on the runway waiting in line for our turn to take off. We left the ground at 0732 and flew south over the Guadalcanal mountains to avoid the worst weather, then turned west to Esperance. We went up the south coast of Bougainville, traveling the top of cumulus clouds through saddlebacks at 13,000 to 14,000 feet. We hit the front up to 30,000 feet and flew west-southwest for an hour and turned back at 17,000 feet to Treasury Island and then toward Kahili.

Our number three engine began smoking and throwing oil badly. I immediately feathered the engine at 16,000 feet over the target. Junior shouted, "Bombs away," and our frag cluster bombs were dropped at 1143. The bombs hit a Jap housing area with intense concentration coming from a 75 mm gun. In total we had 75 120-pound frag bombs hit our target. We returned to the base with a seven-to-10-mile-visibility landing at 1400.

Gorsuch, Fitz and I got out inspecting the damaged number three engine. It had blown the cylinder head up and the cowling had buckled and pulled out the studs. We were lucky to make it back with that kind of damage.

Major Dewey came to our hut to inform Fitz and Leo Hunt, "You two bastards are captains as of December 14th." Hunt passed out cigars. This evening we went to the movie to see "Watch on the Rhine." However, the movie had to be stopped due to all the rain. We walked back across the suspension foot bridge and had our second briefing on the Rabaul mission.

December 19, 1943 Sunday
Raid Lakunai Airdrome at Rabaul

Our briefing was the night before as we got up this morning at 0530. The ship we flew then, number 261, was having the engine changed so we were assigned plane number 268. The ground crews had just fixed oxygen leaks in the ball and top turrets.

Major Zinn's ship was out so we followed Colonel Burnham and took off at 0840. Eight out of our 10 planes got off the runway as we flew under the front at 1,000 feet to the Russell's. We flew north of Bougainville at 17,000 feet to avoid the fronts. When we approached Kieta we circled then flew through to Empress Augusta Bay to pick up our 48 fighter escorts, consisting of P38s, P-40s, F-40s and F6F's.

The colonel had to turn back due to a gas leak so we took the lead. We were over the target at 20,500 feet with high cumulus clouds over the mountains. The runway had been obscured until we were on top of it so we dropped into the supply and dock areas. Two large AKs (cargo ships) were on fire and exploded. We also saw several Zeros taking off from the Lakuani strip. Two of them made a pass coming at us but quickly pulled out of range as our 50-caliber guns cut loose on them.

There were over 30 dogfights over the 31st Squadron flying in the number two position. The squadron had dropped 103 bombs on the strip as the fighters protected us as best they could. The Zeros were making attacks at the belly of our bombers as the ball turret and nose gunners opened fire. Our fighter cover was exceptionally good; however, five P-38s, five F6Fs and two F-40s were lost. One F-40 crashed head on with a Zero.

We headed for home with the fighters going back to Cherry Blossom, one of the fighter airstrips. We had bad weather all the way home, flying at 1,500 feet and landing at 1630.

December 20, 1943 Monday

We have another strike on Rabaul scheduled for Tuesday morning and had the briefing that night at 1900. I received a few more records in the mail from mother. A few were broken in the flight over here but we were able to salvage "Oh, What a Beautiful Morning."

December 21, 1943 Tuesday

We were up at 0500 and would be taking plane number 812, Droopsnoot. At 0720 we took off and noticed that our generators were on the blink. The 31st Squadron peeled off only to land shortly after takeoff. The mission had been cancelled due to bad weather.

A flying boot was caught in our nose wheel door and the wheel wouldn't go down. We landed behind the 31st after getting the wheel fixed. Another plane with hidden problems! The colonel came back and stopped in for some ice cream.

December 22, 1943 Wednesday
Munda, New Georgia

Our orders had been changed and we were assigned plane number 826. The plane was loaded with six 1,000-pound demo bombs. We would take off the next morning to hit a convoy north of New Ireland. We took off at 1300 and landed back on Cactus at 1510.

Colonel Pritchard, of Bomber Command, briefed the crews for the strike on Rabaul airdrome. Possible targets mentioned were Kunakanu, Lakunai or Simpson Harbor shipping. We had to mentally prepare ourselves for another raid. Between the weather and raids being cancelled and briefings for upcoming missions it began to wear on your nerves. I could usually gauge the tension by watching Fitz. He was a bundle of nerves. I also knew that once we were in the air he would calm down and do what needed to be done. I knew that some of the best ways to handle these situations was with a good sense of humor. Sometimes, it was difficult to find anything funny to laugh at; however you needed some diversion from these ongoing strikes.

December 23, 1943 Thursday
Raid on Lakunai, Rabaul

The morning's raid on Rabaul got underway when two squadrons of B-24s took off at 0955. Each of our bombers was loaded with six 1,000-pound bombs. We flew to our rendezvous location of Torokina where we met up with 22 B-26s and 48 fighters at an altitude of 15,000 feet.

We proceeded to Walton Island at 21,000 feet and were intercepted by some Zeros just before our run. They were over us dropping phosphorous aerial bombs, hoping to hit us and have the chemical start eating through the metal which might cause our planes to weaken and crash.

There were about 30 Zeros over Simpson Harbor and the ack-ack was heavy, hitting our lead plane in the wing and through its gas tank, draining the gas from the number two engine. We saw them feather their engine. Lieutenant Robertson was pilot, flying lead in the second element. His bombardier, Lieutenant J.D. Robertson, was shot through the head with a 7.7 mm shell, killing him instantly. His co-pilot from the 31st Squadron was hit in the chest with a 7.7 mm shell and had a slug of shrapnel in him so Robertson, the pilot, peeled off and headed for Munda.

Zinner's ship was also shot up and had to land on Munda. Captain Hunt in his ship, Balls O'Fire, claimed shooting down four Zeros.

The aerial bombs were bursting very near us as we continued on course to our target. Our squadrons were able to drop 138 1,000-pound bombs over the target at 1327. The number of Jap Zeros ripped from the sky totaled 30. We lost four of our fighters on this mission, which was rated good.

On our return, we flew by Empress Augusta, Munda and landed at Koli airstrip on Cactus at 1730 after seven and a half hours of flight time. When we landed, Fitz had commented how glad he was to be back home after witnessing all those dogfights.

Chapter 23

December 24, 1943 Friday Christmas Eve
Munda, New Georgia

We were giving up another plane, number 826, and had to transfer our equipment to plane number 268 for our next trip to Munda. We took off from Koli Airfield at 1300 and landed at 1530. A P-38 was landing right behind us with one of his engines shot out.

Some of us guys went over to the 73rd's Seabees where we traded a quart and a half of whiskey for six Jap shell cups. Garman got his knife and ashtrays in part of the trade. Whiskey is being bootlegged up to $100 per quart.

A briefing was held at 2000 for the strike on Rabaul Saturday. It felt as if this war would never end. The crew had been unusually quiet going about their duties. I supposed they were wondering like me, how much more of this we could endure. Maybe it was just because it was Christmas Eve and we were all lonesome and missed our loved ones back home.

There was a Christmas tree on the hill top put up by a Negro outfit. The night sky was clear, beautiful and full of bright stars. Back in the barracks there is lots of singing—"White Christmas" and "Pistol Packin' Mama."

December 25, 1943 Saturday
Raid on Rabaul; Lakunai

Christmas morning. We were up at 0500 with breakfast in the mess at 0530. Gorsuch and Wainman came running in and ran up to the rest of the crew. Gorsuch was smiling ear-to-ear and appeared to be out of breath. "Captain, we've got her! We've got her back!" Wainman was laughing and was equally excited as he shouted, "This is the best Christmas gift!"

Bill Garman said, "You guys have been up kinda early this morning, why don't you get some coffee."

Fitz at the same time said, "Got who back?"

Almost in unison they exclaimed,

"Scootin' Thunder! She's sitting on the field and the CO has given her back to us, I mean you."

I quickly answered, "No, you had it right the first time; us."

Garman was still a bit skeptical and said, "Have you guys been drinking egg-nog?"

"No Lieutenant, look at the flight schedule." Gorsuch handed the schedule to Fitz as I peered over his shoulder. Gorsuch read out loud, "Ship number 4240100 is assigned to Captain Fitzhenry and crew."

All the guys jumped from their seats cheering like they were at a football game. Fitz sat there stunned looking at the flight schedule.

I patted him on the shoulder and said, "We've got a raid on Rabaul this morning, what do ya say we Scoot on out of here?" Fitz jumped from his seat and it was clear to see the sudden change in his mood. He was all smiles like a kid with a new toy.

Fitz looked at his watch and said, "We're taking off at 0800. I've got a plane to check out. You guys get your gear and get over to the field as soon as possible. Bob, Clincher and Junior, let's go." It was still dark outside as we made our way to one of the jeeps. I drove with Fitz in the passenger seat. I thought I should drive since the news of getting our plane back was still having an effect on him.

I drove to the field in a drizzling cold rain as we pulled up to the revetment and stopped 20 feet from her. "She looks great," said Garman.

Junior added, "Wow, can you believe it?" The rain was steady as Fitz and I got out of the jeep, grabbed our canteens and headed for our plane. The rain stopped almost as suddenly as it had started. There was a distant cracking of thunder as Fitz and I stood for a moment looking at her nose art, the lightning bolt piercing the moon and her name emblazoned on each side.

I looked at Fitz and gave him a gentle shove and said, "Whad'ya know? Looks like Santa Claus answered your wish."

He laughed and said, "Yeah, we must have been very good."

I took his bag and gear to put on board as he began his walk around the plane. Another jeep pulled up and Gorsuch, Wainman, Noland and Mattson jumped off. Gorsuch did the walk around with Fitz as I kept my eye out for our two other guys. Jones and Lawson hitched a ride on the next jeep pulling onto the airfield. The lads were all smiles as they stowed their gear and prepared for takeoff.

It had been a while since I'd seen all our crew this happy. I glanced at my watch; it was 0555 on Christmas morning. I zipped up my jacket against the cold and wet. We were standing in the rain getting ready for our 39th combat mission; target Rabaul. I thought for a moment, I'm sure it must be snowing in Indiana today. However, I'm glad to be right here, this moment with this crew of guys. I can't think of a better gift, aside from landing safely back here after this mission.

We left at 0800, assembling the group over the Limbo Island at 0930. We picked up our fighter escorts at 1050 near Torokina. We would have 64 fighters on the mission; P-38 Lightnings, F-40 Wildcats, F6F Hellcats and P-40 Warhawks.

We encountered thunderheads up to 35,000 feet between Buka and New Britain so we went to Green Islands and across to New Ireland to hit our I/P of Lakunai. We released our bombs at 1200 and turned for home. Major Zinn's ship was hit and the bomb bay doors jammed so the bombs wouldn't release. He chopped off power at 23,000 feet and the rest of the squadron overran the sky and it was full of vagrant airplanes. Our tail gunner, Mattson, said he had to pull in the guns to keep from being hit by another ship.

Twenty Zeros were attacking us from above dropping phosphorous aerial bombs at very close range. We cut through saddleback holes across the 72nd formation and tacked on a left wing at 200 miles per hour dodging the cloudy strings raining down on us.

One P-38 was shot accidentally and with one wheel down. He stuck with the bombers for protection. I looked out the cockpit window to my right and saw the P-38 Lightning, just under our wing. I waved to the pilot and he gave me a thumbs-up. Scootin' Thunder gave him cover until his landing strip came into view and he peeled off away from us. We heard one fighter pilot yelling over the radio, "Merry Christmas, Tojo, you slant-eyed sumuvva bitch!"

We flew back to Munda alone landing at 1630 with just 300 gallons of fuel remaining. Three other Liberators with wounded aboard, landed just after us. Lieutenant Sam D'Ambruoso gave first aid and had blood all over his T-shirt. One man had 20 pieces of steel in his head and back but was not critical. Major Zinn landed at Koli back on Cactus. The report back from the mission indicated we had 15 B-24s over the target and four over Kahili. Eight planes did not reach the primary target. A total of 103 1,000-pound bombs were dropped and 17 salvoed over the water while 12 returned with their ships.

Colonel Unruh gave a party in the club from 1730 until 2030 with free champagne and sparkling burgundy. We all got very drunk and returned to our barracks on all instruments. All the crew was thrilled to have Scootin' Thunder back. She had performed admirably and we felt protected and invincible while flying our ship once again. It might just have been all the beer or rum and Cokes talking. I'm not sure, but I did notice the change in our crew once we got her back. It was as if everything was going to be OK, just keep working together like we always have and our plane will take care of the rest.

For the moment I was completely relaxed and thought…this is probably the best Christmas I've ever had. I spent it with my nine brothers…What a day!

December 26, 1943 Sunday

We had fresh eggs for breakfast. Colonel Reddoch gave the Air Medal to Richardson, Tiemann, Mann, Gerry Cass and me. He told us that as of December 23rd, 58 Zeros had been shot down.

December 27, 1943 Monday

The squadron has been alerted to be on standby. Two Jap battleships, heavy cruisers and destroyer's were near and we might have to leave for Kavieng.

I got some additional transition time, flying from 1300 to 1500 with rain closing in. I made two takeoffs and landings in cross winds.

December 28, 1943 Tuesday
Munda, New Georgia

There was another strike on Rabaul being planned for the next day. Our briefing took place at 1045. We took off in Scootin' Thunder at 1315, landing at Munda at 1500. Major Zinn flew with us to Munda. We also had a Bomb Command flight surgeon, Major Smith, on board with us again. We were carrying a load of four 1,000-pound bombs and some bomb bay tanks to be used on other planes at Munda.

We got a late lunch and went to our quarters for some rest. It rained all day and provided a pleasant backdrop with the steady pelting of rain on the Quonset hut's roof. It was perfect for some much-needed sleep.

December 29, 1943 Wednesday

We were up at 0500 and ready for our 0830 takeoff. However, the relentless rain cancelled our mission. At 0300 the air raid sirens went off, causing several of us to run out of the barracks into the pouring rain. Timo managed to scurry past everyone and was standing in the mud looking like a drowned rat. That boy was a bundle of nerves.

December 30, 1943 Thursday
Strike on Malai Village in the Shortland Group

It was an overcast morning on Munda as we took off at 0740. Fitz didn't check the manifold pressure and number four waste-gate valve stuck shut. We cut back quickly and braked to stop and to taxi back. Gorsuch adjusted the waste-gates and discovered the number two supercharger was out and we had a gas leak. We called Bomb Command for a new target as we got underway with Scootin' Thunder on our second takeoff at 1030. We were ordered to hit the Malai Village near Shortland along with 26 B-26s.

We came in over the target at 13,000 feet and encountered light ack-ack which just missed us. Junior sighted and gave the command, "Bombs away," at 1123. The bombs hit 200 yards left of the village on a compass heading of 338 degrees.

Several of our ships were shot at Rabaul by 80–100 Zeros. The squadron shot down 14 Zeros with the help of our 48 fighter escorts. They managed to destroy 12 more Zekes which flew in groups of five. We got 90 1,000-pound bombs hitting the target as Garman shouted, "Do a 180 and get the hell out of here."

Just ahead and to our right the Pretty Prairie Special had been hit and her bomb bay door fell off with an engine smoking. Colonel Unruh's plane signaled with his wings for the number two plane to take over the lead. The Colonel immediately went into cloud cover at 12,000 feet.

First Lieutenant Tony Kuhn, Wilson's bombardier, was flying his first mission since his water landing with Wilson. He was acting as group bombardier for the colonel. Also on board was Major Frederick Koebig, the navigator. We lost sight of the Colonel but it appeared he had control of the Pretty Prairie Special as she was descending rapidly.

Captain Leo Hunt got three 20 mm shells in his bomb bay as his squadron shot down 10 Zeros. Major Zinn's number two engine was shot out. The rest of our squadron returned to Koli Field to assess any other damage to our planes. Everyone was asking, "Did you see the colonel and his ship go into the clouds? Did anyone see anything else?" We all felt an immediate sense of loss.

0419-6000

BOARDING PASS

REMSBURG/CLARK

NO FF CREDIT

FLIGHT	DATE		SEAT
DL314	14AUG		11B

ORIGIN: ATLANTA
DESTINATION: PORTLAND ME

ZONE 4

OPERATED BY DELTA AIR LINES INC

BAGS 01

▲ DELTA

BOARDING PASS

REMSBURG/CLARK

2 006 2179327256 0

NO FF CREDIT

FLIGHT	DATE	CLASS	ORIGIN		SEAT
DL314	14AUG	N	ATLANTA		11B

OPERATED BY: COACH
DESTINATION: PORTLAND ME
DELTA AIR LINES INC

DEPARTURE GATE — SEE AIRPORT MONITORS

ZONE 1

PAGE 01

Chapter 24

December 31, 1943 Friday
Search mission for Colonel Unruh and crew

A big tree fell at 0300 slamming onto the ground near the barracks on Koli Field. It got everyone up and out of bed. We thought it might have been some Jap bogey bombers sneaking through the night. We slept for another hour and got going at 0400, getting dressed and fed and out to the airstrip. Major McKinley would be leading a party consisting of five B-24s in the search for Colonel Unruh and the crew of the Pretty Prairie Special.

We loaded our gear onto Scootin' Thunder and took off in the dark at 0600. The place they were last sighted was near the Kilinailau Islands. The sun was coming up as we came in low over some of the native outriggers and buzzed several of the islands, keeping a sharp look out for our downed comrades. Fitz was taking pictures along the way. We sighted two spouted water explosions which might have been a sub or a sonic mine.

We turned and headed for Green Island when we were intercepted by a PB4Y already over Green Island, also looking for the missing crew. We started down the New Ireland coast at Cape Bun Bun when Wainman and Gorsuch shouted out, "I see them! They're on the beach." I looked out the cockpit window and saw the guys waving a parachute to get our attention.

Fitz dropped down to 50 feet and circled to get a better look. Sure enough, there they were, eight of them visible on the beach. It looked like the colonel on the left side standing near a tree. We circled again coming in at 30 feet and our guys kept shouting, "We found them, there they are!" We counted only eight men; two were missing.

Fitz steered Scootin' Thunder around for the third time with Richardson's and McKinley's planes just behind us. We were coming in very low, about 15 feet off the ground. As we circled and got close to them, our crew dropped supplies and survival equipment. Richardson's and McKinley's crews did likewise. We saw the men run out from the beach for the supplies as we pulled up and away. The colonel stayed put near the trees while the crew scrambled to retrieve the supplies.

It was a dangerous situation. We had to drop the supplies and try not to bring attention to the guys stranded on the beach. It's kind of difficult to disguise three B-24s coming in at a very low altitude and throwing things to the men below. We didn't know if the Japs were in the area looking for the survivors too.

We pulled up and got out of there as Fitz excitedly struggled over the radio, giving verbal position to the base. He finally got it through as we headed for home in rotten weather. There were violent updrafts and thunderheads as we made our way home in the pouring rain.

We landed at Koli on Guadalcanal at 1430. The last we heard was that two Dumbos (rescue planes) were sent from Torokina. We went to the club that night, in the pouring rain, for a couple of beers. It was New Year's Eve and no one felt like celebrating. What an awful way to bring in the New Year.

Everyone was hopeful Unruh and his crew would be picked up and returned as soon as possible.

January 1, 1944 Saturday
New Year's Day.

The news back home said we had air superiority over Rabaul. It was quite a different story when you saw 80 Zeros spitting 20 mm shells at you up there. However, we had just been informed that we wouldn't be relieved until the tactical situation at Rabaul, New Britain, eased up.

The 307th lost a ship over Rabaul and two made crash landings at Torokina on Bougainville. There was no word yet whether they'd picked up Colonel Unruh and his crew from New Ireland. I know crews would be sent to keep searching as long as we can. No one would give up the search after having seen them on the beach. I could only imagine their fear and disappointment in not being picked up the first time we spotted them.

January 2, 1944 Sunday
Munda, New Georgia

I flew pilot to Munda with Don Robertson co-piloting. Robertson was to be flown to Torokina by TBF to go on a Dumbo PBY search for Colonel Unruh and crew on the New Ireland coast. The word at Munda was that we'd hit the shipping at Kavieng, New Ireland, with takeoff set for 0230 in the morning.

A Navy lad who rode with us, Peter Marich of San Francisco, promises us some filet steaks from the USS Matsonia on which he is the butcher.

Our briefing got started at 1900 for a 0230 takeoff to hit two damaged Jap heavy cruisers at Kavieng Harbor, New Ireland. We were to fly in the number two position on Major Zinn's right wing. Zinn would not be flying and McKinley was scheduled to replace him as the lead plane.

January 3, 1944 Monday
Raid on Kavieng, New Ireland
Shipping Harbor

Combat mission number 42 got underway with us taking off from the Munda Air Field at 0217. We were settled in Scootin' Thunder, with all engines revving at maximum speed. We waited for our turn to race down the runway with the aid of lights and a searchlight beam illuminating the strip. Each one of our planes was loaded with four 1,000-pound bombs as we barely cleared the trees at the scant flying speed. We are flying on instruments and AFCE (Automatic Flight Control Equipment) with a 300-degree compass heading to Simberi Island at dawn, 0632.

We circled until 0705, picking up only two of the 394$^{th's}$ ships and three new crews of the 72nd. The P-38s were scheduled to pick us up on the way home from the target. We led six ships to the I/P. At 0732 we were at an altitude of 9,000 feet, when Fitz said to Junior, "You've got her." Junior sighted and exclaimed, "Bombs away," and we broke away and turned for home.

We turned for home and looked down at the airstrip below. We could see the Zeros zipping off the runway, creating small clouds of dust from our perspective. We knew in a heartbeat they were coming up after us. Garman was taking movies and Fitz and I stayed focused on the sky around us, looking for intruders.

At nearly the same time, 0740, there was a fighter sweep on Rabaul and the radio chatter was high. It turned out that one of the Marine fighter pilots that we heard shouting was Major Greg "Pappy" Boyington. He had been with the "Flying Tigers" in China and was now in the Pacific as the commander of the Marine Fighter Squadron 214. The major was flying an F4U Corsair that the Japanese called, "Whistling Death," (Boyington and his squadron had shot down several enemy fighters and he was awarded the Navy Cross and later would receive the Congressional Medal of Honor by President Truman.)

This morning he was shot down and ejected from his plane at 0745. He managed to inflate his raft and climbed inside severely wounded and was later captured by the Japanese.

The Zeros chasing our formation were hanging on in the most persistent fight we had had to date. Our gunners used almost all their ammunition in a running 65-minute fight with us traveling at only 165 miles per hour. The sound of all our machine guns firing together was deafening. Spent cartridges bounced all over the inside of the ship. The Zeros had belly tanks and pursued us for what felt like an eternity. Leo Hunt's plane, Balls O'Fire, was hit and badly damaged.

We finally saw 16 of our P-38s come into view and race past us to attack the Zeros. When we were close enough to an airstrip near Bougainville, we buzzed the field and shot a flare to clear the way for Hunt to land. He brought his ship down landing at Torokina, with his number four engine feathered and number three leaking oil rapidly. He landed with a flat tire but everyone was OK. We sorely missed the fighter escorts that had followed Colonel Reddoch to Kahili as we burned up 2,300 gallons of fuel.

The Zeros had made coordinated attacks mostly from high and above and from the front quarters, over on their backs shooting into our formation, then back to the right side up and plunging right among the formation. They looked like brand-new Zeros and very nasty.

We came in for a landing at 1230 with our wheels hitting Henderson Field and creating the familiar noise and vibration of the rubber against the metal of the Marston mats. Major Zinn crash-landed right behind us. His tail gunner was shot in the foot and his bombardier had facial abrasions. Our aerial was shot off. One of the ships from the 72nd needed three new props.

Our waist gunner, Lawson, claimed one probable Zero.

Youngheim of the 72nd and Lieutenant Sentell of the 394th refused to take off that morning because of the weather. Their future was hanging in the balance.

We had nine planes take off and only six made it over the target, releasing 24,000 pounds of explosives. We rode the trucks back to the barracks exhausted and hungry. When I made it to my cot, I forgot my hunger, took off my shoes and fell asleep. We logged 11 hours and 15 minutes of flight time.

No news yet on Colonel Unruh and his crew.

January 4, 1944 Tuesday

Fitz had been assigned the operations officer and McKinley up to commanding officer, supplanting Major Zinn. The Major was going to Auckland and then leave for home with his hay fever trouble. We had been alerted that day about a "mystery" target and were scheduled for a 1500 takeoff, destination Munda.

January 5, 1944 Wednesday
Munda, New Georgia
Tonolei Harbor Mission

Colonel Burnham had presented medals the day before. I got the first cluster to the Air Medal. Our target was Kavieng Harbor shipping; however, it didn't materialize so we settled for some ack-ack positions in the Tonolei Harbor on Bougainville.

We took off from Munda at 0905 and soon realized the target was closed in due to the bad weather so we returned to Guadalcanal with a full bomb load. We logged five hours of flight time and landed at 1410.

January 6, 1944 Thursday

I was checked out as a first pilot today by Commanding Officer Captain McKinley, and Lieutenant Stanley Pietuch rode along. I flew instruments, flare beam, and landed.

Leo Hunt and his crew buzzed the camp area and probably will be reprimanded severely.

January 7, 1944 Friday

Sam D'Ambruoso got his captaincy this evening. There was a meeting at operations to warn against buzzing the area. I had heard 20 rumors to that date that my orders to go home were in Bomber Command. There was also an ugly rumor they had 300 to 500 Jap fighters waiting for us at Rabaul for our strike Saturday. This was very unsettling news after what we went through on January 3rd striking Kavieng. I hoped we would get more fighter coverage this time.

January 8, 1944 Saturday
Rabaul

I was up at 0645, dressed and had breakfast and was at the trucks by 0730. Fitz made his final inspection of the plane with Gorsuch and we waited in line, taking off at 0901. There would be 21 B-26s leading the 394th Squadron as we climbed to 21,000 feet over Torokina. I waited until we started our climb from 12,000 feet before putting on oxygen. We got about 50 miles from Rabaul but since all the fighters didn't show up the 72nd, led by Pierce in the number one position, turned back for Cactus.

The weather had closed in over Poporang, our alternate target, so we flew for home logging seven hours and landing at 1500. McKinley, Fitz, Colonel Reddoch, etc. flew to Munda for a huge bull session with the fighter boys. There was much wailing and gnashing of teeth!

The Rabaul mission was slated for the next day.

The briefing was held at 2100 for the Rabaul strike. Later the strike was cancelled by VF command. It had been raining all day. We wouldn't fly however, as Fitz traded positions with McKinley.

Leo Hunt, Garman and Timo argued viciously over bombing run technique for hours. At first it was amusing to see Clincher go after the gremlin. However, these guys wouldn't back down from their positions at all and just kept it going. I returned to my pipe and book and blocked them out.

January 10, 1944 Monday

The squadron took off individually, starting at 1815 to hit Rabaul on a harassing mission. I was tower officer since our crew didn't fly. I was there from midnight to 0800. All the boys got back OK, reporting they had effective hits with the frags and 500-pound demos with parachutes. They did not encounter any interception by the Japs. McKinley had dropped through the clouds on a time run.

Later in the day I filled out a B-24 questionnaire with the aid of Stanley Pietuch. Stanley read the questions to me and they were all pretty basic and easy enough considering all the hours I had logged flying one of these boxcars.

January 11, 1944 Tuesday

Youngheim's co-pilot, Robison, is being groomed to take over the crew. Sentell, the 394th pilot who balked on a recent raid, received promotion to first lieutenant despite his actions of a few days ago. Apparently, the promotion had come through before his refusal to fly. We have also heard that our record six-ship mission to Kavieng will get Distinguished Flying Crosses for pilot, navigator and bombardier. As co-pilot, I was put in for Air Medal. That had to be an oversight as we were all on the same missions together.

Chapter 25

January 12, 1944 Wednesday

The briefing began at 1600 for the Rabaul mission scheduled for Thursday. We would be in the first ship of the 394th to take off at 2209, thereafter at six-minute intervals. We were on course as we climbed to 8,000 feet. Fitz gave the controls over to me as we flew along the southern coast of Santa Isabel and through the Manning Straits at 2330.

At 0025 I saw what seemed to be furious shelling towards Shortland, about 80 degrees to port. Ice was forming on the turrets and the bombardier's glass at 21,000 feet.

Fitz was back at the wheel on our approach and turned left instead of right as Clincher had said over the interphone. Searchlights caught us immediately right over Lakunai and Garman told Junior to "Let'em go," at 0210 January 13th, our 45th combat mission.

Once we were clear of enemy territory the crew could relax and unwind. The view of the tranquil sky on the way home was magnificent. The stars dotted the sky with a full moon illuminating our plane against a nearly cloudless backdrop. Instead of reaching for a cigar, I sang the song that fit with the beautiful scenery…

"It must have been moon glow, way up in the blue. It must have been moon glow that led me straight to you…We seemed to float right through the air. Heavenly songs seemed to come from everywhere."

We landed Scootin' Thunder at 0520 back on Cactus and I slept until lunch.

There was a funeral at 1400 for Lieutenant Kenneth Haines, a co-pilot from the 23rd. His legs were severed in a freak landing accident on January 12th on Carney Field. The ship blew a tire on landing and in the twist tore through other landing gear. The prop broke and cut through the co-pilot's side of the ship cutting off his legs and causing him to bleed to death. He had survived a combat mission only to die when they came in for a landing.

A Jap plane followed a snooper plane into Munda last night and laid a string of bombs across the runway damaging about seven planes.

January 14, 1944 Friday

It had been raining all day. We wouldn't be flying; however, a briefing was held at 1500 for another strike on Rabaul. Most of the Liberators took off but several returned because of the heavy fronts en route. Five ships got through to the target at Rabaul, returned and landed at Munda. Later in the evening we had another bull session in the barracks as the rain continued to pound away.

January 15, 1944 Saturday

I traded McKinley three cigars for intelligence that my orders to go home were here and ready to be delivered. Whatta feeling!

Leo Hunt took off from Munda in the morning twice before he made it through the weather. His bombs hit the corner of a town in Rabaul. All the crews are in from Munda with the weather being the worst of the semester. The ships had to be brought in on radar.

I rode to the 21st Evacuation Hospital to see our nose gunner, Red Noland. He may need an operation for appendicitis.

January 16, 1944 Sunday

My orders to go home were OK'd but wouldn't be ready until January 23rd. Until then, I was officially grounded by the 5th Group.

It rained like hell all day. There was a river right by the door of the Quonset hut with a mammoth banyan tree hanging precariously over the hut, which had us all on edge. The limb fell off in a high gale and had everybody headlong outside.

January 17, 1944 Monday

Colonel Burnham went to the 307th. He and Colonel Reddoch drank more than somewhat at the officers club and ended up filibustering on each side of the club. Chief Riggs called us away from the crap table twice to listen to nonsense speeches.

Al "Kahili" Cohen gave me luck by proffering an occasional drink and cigar. He asked me if I was "part of the gang at Kavieng? And does the service make you nervous?" Back home at 2300.

January 18, 1944 Tuesday

Garman, Harris, Pietuch, Lieutenant Ablett and Tiemann got Air Medals and clusters today. Adams, Lieutenant Horne and Lieutenant Smith of the 72nd got DFC's while Lieutenant Davy O'Brien got only Air Medal for the Kavieng strike of November 1943, another travesty of justice in the award system.

News was that our crews, who got through to Rabaul through the bad weather the other night, would get the DFC. That meant all of us! Leo Hunt rejoiced.

Back in the barracks there was a heated discussion on religion between Fitz and Sammy D, whom we call "That Damn Bruoso!" (D'Ambruoso). "Which is the greater sin, stealing a man's last $1,000 or $1,000 from a millionaire?"

January 19, 1944 Wednesday

It rained all night but the sun came out for the first time in a week. I am reading *A Farewell to Arms* aloud to Hunt, Timo and Garman. In the afternoon I took a picture of the Malimbu River with Clincher.

January 20, 1944 Thursday

My crew flew their first strike without me. Lieutenant Kreined flew as co-pilot. The squadron took off at 0700. The bombers made a feint on Rabaul to suck the Zeros off the ground then turned back to hit Kahili while our fighters went in for a sweep at Rabaul. The guys landed at 1400. They told me about a B-25 pilot who took off from Sterling in a fit of passion and strafed Rabaul after the formation turned back due to the bad weather. The rumor is he will be decorated, then court-martialed.

January 21, 1944 Friday

Fitz flew to New Ireland on a strike hitting the ack-ack batteries at Boropop. There was a huge push at the club celebrating the end of the strike period. Major Dewey came over to raise hell because of the noise.

January 22, 1944 Saturday

The 23rd Squadron took over the strike duties on the night mission to Rabaul dropping incendiaries. The boys of the 72nd were packing for Auckland and some R&R. Fitz, Clincher, Junior and the other enlisted guys would leave in the morning and were getting their gear in order. The other lads from our crew, Gorsuch, Wainman, Noland, Mattson, Jones and Lawson, stopped by the hut to say goodbye and to wish me well. We all stopped and had a drink and laughed about me being the lucky one to be the first to get out of this mud hole.

As corny as it may sound, I was going to miss these guys. We were more than just a bunch of guys randomly thrown together to navigate these flying boxcars. We were a crew. We successfully completed 45 combat missions always working together as a team, always looking out for each other, the way brothers protect each other. We are the original crew of our B-24: Scootin' Thunder.

I kept the mood light, as did the others with lots of laughing; shaking hands and plans to stay in touch when we all returned to our homes in the States. Fitz seemed more quiet than usual.

When the guys were leaving to go back to their barracks I waved to them and shouted, "Stay safe, guys!" They echoed back, "You too, Lieutenant."

January 23, 1944 Sunday

Fitz and the crew would be taking off at 0700 in Scootin' Thunder. The crew would catch a C-47 at Carney Field, for their third trip to New Zealand. I went out to the tower to say goodbye to Dan Byrne and watch some of the other Liberators take off for Carney. There was Fyrtle Myrtle, Shamrock, Tim-ber, Big Chief, Mary Lou, Balls O'Fire and Fuzzy Wuzzy, racing down the airstrip before pulling up to clear the banyan trees at the end of the 3,000-foot runway.

I stared at the end of the runway at the last ship to take off. She was turning onto the strip and braked with full throttle on her engines. Fitz held her there for a moment longer then moved his feet off the brakes and Scootin' Thunder peeled off down the runway with the familiar drone of her engines racing past me and then lifting off and into the air. It felt awkward viewing her from this angle, all the while feeling like I should be aboard at the controls with Fitz.

I felt a clutch in my throat and swallowed hard as they flew out of sight. I looked over at Dan and smiled with pride. Dan said something about the ships would be heading back for another strike on Rabaul and the 31st Squadron would be leading the way. I heard the approaching sound of a Liberator circling back and over head. I was standing in the tower when Scootin' Thunder came back to buzz the field. I'm sure this was Fitz's way of saying goodbye for now as he tipped his wings and pulled her back and I watched until they disappeared from view. I smiled a huge grin and thought a silent wish that all the lads would get to go home soon and leave this war behind them.

January 24, 1944 Monday

Garman, Harris and Hunt's crew took off for Auckland. In the evening I went to the officers club and won some $250 at the craps table. This brings my winnings to $760, total cash on hand: $960. There were numerous goodbyes being spoken as I headed back to my barracks a bit richer and feeling a bit buzzed.

January 25, 1944 Tuesday

Slept most of the day. Lights went out and we had a bull session in the hut. Lieutenant MacMillian, from Nashville, Tennessee, dropped by.

January 26, 1944 Wednesday

Lieutenants Tom Hayden, Dick Holdeman, John Allsbury and John Freel made a water landing near Outong Java skirting a front, returning from the Rabaul mission. Lieutenant Morton's crew made a crash landing at Sterling with at least one officer killed. Lieutenant Daugherty's crew also made a water landing; nothing had been heard about their situation yet. Hayden's crew reported they had been picked up. Rumor had it that Fitz has been transferred to the 23rd operations. Drinks at the club.

January 27, 1944 Thursday

I went to the beach and then the club for special services to exchange records and books. I then went to the finance office to get my pay.

January 28, 1944 Friday

The camp area is almost deserted. McKinley, Ablett, "Kahili" Cohen, Lieutenant Tom Thompson all left for Auckland in the morning. The 13 Air Force Band played at the theatre that night. I went to the club with Robertson for a few rum and Cokes. Hayden's crew got back from their latest mission and all are OK. One of the gunners got a broken rib, the only injury. They landed at 85 miles per hour. Two of the 307th crews had water landings and would go to Auckland the next day instead of Robertson.

January 29, 1944 Saturday

I slept very late. No mail again. I went to the APO 709 Post Office to get my stuff censored but no censor was there. I went back to my hut and started packing. Later in the evening I went to the club for drinks, then home in the rain with Lieutenant Larsen. All three of us ducked under Robertson's raincoat.

January 30, 1944 Sunday

Robertson and Lieutenant Brandon flew to Auckland. The mess was a shabby affair these days with no more than a dozen in the hall at any time. I wrote seven or eight letters informing the folks at home not to write. The rain continued to pour all night. I had a chat with Tom Hayden and John Allsbury after their water landing.

January 31, 1944 Monday

A note: "If there is such a thing as fate, it is not three eerie sisters, with loom and shears. It is an ape throwing dice!" from Benjamin Blake.

I spent another evening at the club for a drink and a cigar. The pounding rain was still the backdrop as I had a bull session with McConnell discussing "The strange woman from Auckland."

Memoranda: Air Medal for June 16 to June 25th; Cluster for June 27 to July 11th; Cluster for July 13 to July 25th.

February 1, 1944 Tuesday

It rained all day. I stayed inside and read. The rain finally got to me and I dozed off in a wonderful slumber. Later in the evening I went out for dinner but hurried back to the warm shelter in our hut.

February 2, 1944 Wednesday

There was gentle rain through the night. I went for a swim at Koli point on Cactus. The waves seemed a mile high pounding into the beach with an undertow that was pulling you out to sea. The hot sun was glaring yet because of the gale you couldn't feel it.

February 3, 1944 Thursday

The river just outside the Quonset hut had risen to the brim of the banks due to the rains. The area just outside the huts had flooded in many places. It was better to stay in the hut than to venture outside into the rain and slide around in the mud.

February 4, 1944 Friday

I drove to the finance office with Nick Vrabel to be paid. I drew $137.71 in pay.

Bud Hagerman, due for his captaincy in two weeks or so, offered majority if he accepts bomber command operations post to stay until July. Gerry Cass turned down the job.

February 5, 1944 Saturday

The club was closed. The outdoor theatre played "Yankee Doodle Dandy." I had a hunch that my orders would be here the next day. I heard that a C-47 troop transport went down Friday between Tontonta and Buttons.

Chapter 26

February 6, 1944 Sunday

Lieutenant Dave Newman, the informer, runs through the camp like an Indian shouting, "They're here," meaning our orders. Hyland called the port director for transportation and got the news that we could go aboard the next morning to United States, direct! Later we heard Major Samelstein only has copy of orders so we'll have to wait three days for copies from Munda. Executive Officer Joe Founds goes to bat and gets copies made here.

I went back to the barracks and began to pack my things in earnest. I drank the last of Clincher's beer and hit the sack after numerous farewells with the lads accompanied by numerous drinks.

February 7, 1944 Monday
Leave for Home!!

I went to the Army port director at Tenaru Beach where I had to wait in the rain for the barge to a Dutch merchant ship, the Kota Baroe. Captain Russey, a sandy-haired transport commander, and the Dutch master, J. Vandermeer situated in a portside stateroom, six of us in a nine-cot cabin. The lucky ones to leave were:

Captain W.C. Wright	Laredo, TX
Captain W.A. Quinn	Saginaw, MI
Captain N.R. West	Chicago, IL
Lt. S.J. Bakula	Niagara Falls, NY
Lt. J.S. Hyland	New Bedford, MA
Lt. Nick Vrabel	Youngstown, OH
Lt. D.M. Newman	Brooklyn, NY
Lt. W.G. Fuller	Fort Worth, TX, and me…
Lt. G.R. Houser	Logansport, IN

In addition, there were three Navy officers; Lt.(S.G.) Calvin P. Chester from Wellsville, MO; Lt. (J.G.) Karl Schwartz from Buffalo, N.Y. and Lt. (J.G.) John Sawula of San Francisco, CA.

All of us thrilled to be on our way home.

February 8, 1944 Tuesday

Two weeks ago, Al "Kahili" Cohen wanted to know where I would be located at 2000 on this night. I had been in Tulagi Harbor watching PBYs land in the fierce rain. Al was a great guy and always very funny. Al had a way to cut through all the tension with his quick wit and great sense of humor. He had said we would reconnect in the States once he was freed from his duty here.

February 9, 1944 Wednesday
Headed for the States.

We got underway at 1215 local time to join a convoy of four other ships, a Republic, a Liberty Ship and two DDs with a southeast heading zigzagging along Southern Malaita at blackout time.

I needed to reset my watch and advance it in a half-hour, at 0300. We had to wear or carry life vests everywhere we went. All of us guys put a dollar into a pool to guess our arrival date. I took March 3, 1944 at 2100. We had only 200 tons of water aboard and rationing was necessary.

February 18, 1944 Friday

Corporal Roy Davenport was released from the hospital and was sent back to Cactus only to find out that Colonel Unruh and his crew had been shot down over New Ireland on December 30, 1943, and had not yet been found. Roy was devastated to hear the news, having worked so closely with the Colonel. He, like all of us, deeply respected Unruh for being a fine gentleman and a strong leader. This information was relayed to me by Bill Garman.

March 3, 1944 Friday

Arrived in San Francisco and got a room at the Drake Wiltshire. It took 26 days by boat to arrive in California. I don't remember who won the bet or cared. I was home. Two days later…

March 5, 1944 Sunday

Bill Garman burst in saying, "Thirty-five hours ago I was on Guadalcanal." Bill had opted to take a plane back to the States. Clincher and I had dinner together at 1830 at the Fairmont Hotel.

March 6, 1944 Monday

Lieutenant Hyland was still up when I got back from Nob Hill so we went to Hamilton Field to get our tickets and orders. Donaldson Gorsuch, our engineer, was there. He was now an officer and I bought him an officer's shirt and gave him $16 that I owed before saying goodbye and good luck.

My orders were to report to Denver, Colorado, by the 8th of March so I caught the train to Denver, boarding at 1730. I slept in the upper berth all the way there.

Once I arrived in Denver I had my orders redirect me to Boca Raton, Florida. In a classification interview I was asked what preference I had for future duty. My immediate response was, "fighters." I was told that the decision would have to come from my new station.

When I arrived my orders were awaiting, which indicated I was going to be sent to Galveston, Texas, to become a flight instructor. This is not what I planned or really desired. I always wanted to be a fighter pilot. Al "Kahili" Cohen was also in Florida and we got dates for the evening at the Olney Inn. It had been great to see Clincher, Gorsuch and now Cohen in a more relaxed environment. We could share our mutual experiences from Guadalcanal and combat but doubted anyone else truly cared or understood.

At the end of April, I had completed my transition flying time in Florida and was cleared to leave the post to catch my train on April 24, 1944. The train took me through Jacksonville and Pensacola with a stop over in New Orleans. There was a 12-hour delay so I went into town for a shave and a haircut. I met up with a Lt. Hawes who was shot down on September 6, 1943, on the Stuttgart raid. His crew had bailed out safely but only he, his pilot and engineer were rescued by the Paris underground.

He really had some interesting stories talking about his seven raids in seven and a half months. I was back on the train at 2000 arriving in Galveston on April 27, 1944, at 0730.

At 1015 I was checking in at the base for processing. I ran into Bill Fuller at mess and got a room with him in the BOQ (Bachelor Officers Quarters). I also happened to run into a member of my cadet class, 43-A, Bob Hallett who just arrived today from New Guinea. He reports that classmates; Dick Heuss, John O'Brien, and Frank Hastings are missing in action in the South Pacific. Paul Gordy, another classmate is now a POW in Germany.

The next few days I spent meeting up with friends and having dinner. Having been away from the niceties of life for so long, I really enjoyed relaxing with friends and having drinks and great conversations. Several times we double-dated and went to some of the local clubs for dancing and drinks.

On the evenings that I got back to my room at the crack of dawn, I often slept late into the morning. I took my summer uniform to a post tailor shop for some alterations. The following morning I had a class regarding weather from 0830 to

1130. I had seen and experienced first-hand all the bad weather the South Pacific could throw at you.

Some of the guys from Guadalcanal had been arriving as their tours have ended. Jim Moore, Cass' co-pilot, and Wicker are also here. Moore is scheduled to go to Atlantic City's redistribution center. I have orders to go on a navigation hop to Maxwell Field in Montgomery, Alabama. I collected my flight pay and mileage from Miami Beach in anticipation of my next move.

May 7, 1944 Sunday

I typed a letter to Colonel B.M. Lloyd, requesting transfer to Fighter Command and volunteering for immediate over-seas service. I couldn't see wasting away my time in Galveston as a flight instructor when I could be using the skills and experience I already had from my tour on Guadalcanal. Nothing in Galveston was holding me there.

I had a surprise when SSgt. Homer "Red" Noland, the nose gunner on Scootin' Thunder, dropped by the BOQ. Red had recently gotten married. He informed me that John Mattson, our tail gunner, also got married. Tom Jones, our waist gunner, spent his leave in Tucson with his girlfriend, Carmen. The kicker came when he told me that Leo Wainman's wife, "Hon", isn't really his wife. He had spent all his allotments and is now dating someone else.

Several months had passed and I felt like a ping-pong ball being bounced from one airfield to another. All my transitional flying time had been completed and my request to become a fighter pilot was turned down. I supposed with all my experience as a B-24 pilot it was more beneficial for me to instruct new cadets. It appeared they needed flight instructors to train new B-24 crews more than to send me off for more training as a fighter pilot.

I was a bit depressed about the decision but had no way out of the situation. I was resigned to the fact I was being sent back to Galveston to instruct some other cadets and my previous experience overseas would be more valuable to these new young guys. I tried to make the best of my stay but kept asking myself: how long will this assignment be—and why Galveston?

May 8, 1944 Monday

I got word from Jim Moore in a letter he received from Jesse Crume; Cass' former bombardier. It read that Bill Robison, Youngheim's former co-pilot, and Red Smith were lost in the Truk raid. I also found out that Major Gerry Cass and his crew of the plane Mary Lou II went down on May 5th. Only two men survived the crash and were rescued from a life raft three days later. They were the co-pilot, Joe Broncato, and Willard Horn, the other pilot. Gerry was the command pilot and was lost when his number two engine was shot out and the wing crumpled. These two survivors were able to parachute out before the plane was engulfed in flames and hit the water.

I was deeply saddened to hear the news about Gerry. We had spent a good deal of time talking in our tents and rehashing various combat missions. Gerry even gave me some transitional flying time when Fitz was busy on another strike and in the hospital in New Zealand. I spent a great deal of time thinking about all the brief acquaintances and friendships I had made on Guadalcanal. So many young men like me. We realized the need and performed our service all with the intent to get back home and restart our lives. I know these guys also thought they would be going home soon. I also knew it would do me no good to dwell on the crashes, attacks and violence I experienced from the co-pilot's seat. I could only wish and hope the other guys would make it home safe and this ugliness would come to an end.

Chapter 27

August 11, 1944 Friday

Lieutenants Dolan and Blair convinced me to go along with them to a USO ping-pong club in Galveston. We walked in and saw several guys in uniform playing ping-pong while the music was blaring in another part of the facility where couples were dancing. We scanned the surroundings and decided to have a seat in the lounge area. Blair went over to a refreshment table and got some drinks for the three of us. All the ping-pong tables were being used and I figured we were going to have to wait for some time to get in a game.

Dolan and I were sitting on a sofa when two young women were walking towards the door on their way to leave. They had to walk down an aisle and pass by one of the busy tables and were headed towards us. I found myself staring at this girl. This girl was gorgeous. I couldn't take my eyes off of her. She was the most beautiful girl I have ever seen. Her hair was dark and shiny and fell to her shoulders. Her eyes were hazel, almost lavender looking, set off by the blue dress she was wearing. Her complexion was like porcelain. This beauty looked to be about 5 feet 7 inches tall, slender and a vision to behold. She and her friend were talking to each other when she looked my way and smiled, then lowered her eyes. I immediately got up from the sofa and walked up to this lovely creature, leaving Dolan saying, "Where are you going?"

I introduced myself. Her friend said, "Hello, I'm Dorothy and this is my friend, Elsa." Her name was Elsa!

Dolan walked up and I introduced him to the girls and we spent the next few hours talking, playing ping-pong and having some soft drinks. Elsa looked at her watch and said she had to be getting home. I had a car and offered to drive them home hoping I could have even more time to talk to her. Dolan excused himself and I proceeded to drive the ladies home.

After helping them in the car I said to Dorothy, "Where shall I take you?"

Elsa spoke up and said, "You can drop me off first, I live the closest."

No, that's not what I wanted to hear. Oh well, I tried to make the best of it. I drove the car to the curb in front of her house and got out to open the door for her. I walked with Elsa up to her porch and she thanked me for a pleasant evening. I knew my time for small talk was rapidly closing in on me. I told her it was my pleasure and quickly added, "Do you think I could get your number? I would like to see you again."

She started up the stairs toward the front door and turned smiling a bit, "Let me think about it. Good night Bob." She waved goodbye to Dorothy then quickly opened the door and went inside. I suddenly felt empty as I walked back to the car.

When I got back to the car, Dorothy said, "Don't be discouraged, she's very young and has turned down several boys."

I answered back, "I'm not one of the boys."

Dorothy said, "Ever since Elsa won the Miss Galveston contest she has been a bit more apprehensive about the attention coming her way."

I responded, "She is Miss Galveston? Really?" I thought to myself, no wonder. I drove a few more blocks as Dorothy filled me in on her best friend. I managed to convince her of my sincerity as I walked her to her front door. Dorothy slipped a piece of paper into my hand with Elsa's number.

Then she said, "Bob, she's a senior in high school and her family recently moved here. Elsa is still not certain of her surroundings."

I asked, "Where is she from?"

Dorothy started up the stairs and turned to me, "She was born in San Antonio, she's my best friend and you make sure you're exceptionally nice to her…I think she likes you, Bob."

I thanked Dorothy and walked back to the car. I looked at the slip of paper as my heart started to pound. I was going to call her first thing tomorrow to invite her out. Then it hit me and I started to laugh. Fitz was right! The prettiest gals are from San Antonio. I had just met one.

The next three and a half months zipped by between work at the airbase and spending all my free time with Elsa. I didn't have time to write in my diary. I had found out that Fitz was back home visiting his folks. I called him on Christmas Eve to wish him and his family a Merry Christmas. The year before at this time we had been in Guadalcanal preparing for a raid on Rabaul and wondering if Colonel Unruh and his crew were ever found. Twelve months later I was engaged and about to get married. I told Fitz I was driving back to Indiana and was getting married to my fiancée, Elsa.

Fitz congratulated me and told me that he recently got engaged to Ruth and they planned a February wedding. I told him how great I felt, everything was coming together and after the wedding I would have to go back to Galveston for a while before being assigned to another post. All the doubts, worries and concerns I had while stationed in Guadalcanal felt like a life-time ago. I had a future with a woman I truly loved. We were married on New Year's Eve, December 31, 1944.

In April 1945 we were passing through Denver on the way to Carlisle, Pennsylvania. Elsa and I went to the Fitzhenrys for dinner and they put us up for the night because of a snowstorm. Elsa and Fitz talked about San Antonio and various landmarks in the city. Fitz told her how, when he was a teenager, he had worked in the produce department of a Piggly-Wiggly store.

Elsa asked him a few questions and then said, "Who was your boss?"

Fitz said, "Pete Garza."

Elsa chuckled, "He's my uncle." Talk about a small world.

Fitz and I went into the kitchen to get drinks for the girls when he said something to me I have heard over and over the rest of my life: "How did an ugly bastard like you wind up with a beautiful woman like her?" I just smiled.

TRANSITION TO
2006

The teenage boy is at a backyard BBQ with his parents and grandparents. They are celebrating his grandmother's 80th birthday. His mother suggests that they go in for cake and ice cream. She takes her parents inside to show them her recent antique purchase; the old table filled with family photos. She asks her dad to call Holden and have him join them.

The grandfather knocks on the boy's bedroom door and enters. The boy is retrieving a sweatshirt and a wrapped birthday gift for his grandmother.

"Is it my imagination or do you have even more airplanes in this room? It's getting to look like a hangar."

The boy laughs, "Yeah, I guess so."

"Holden, are you still thinking about joining the military after high school?"

"I'd like to but mom and dad want me to go to college first."

Holden asks the old man, "Grandpa, would you be upset if I were to choose the Air Force rather than the Marines?"

His grandfather smiled and said, "It's your life son, you need to make that choice for yourself. Holden, let's not keep your grandmother waiting. There's a piece of cake and ice cream downstairs with my name on it." He laughs and turns to leave the room.

As he turns the older man glances at the framed picture over the boy's desk. He stops and moves in to get a closer look. The boy notices his grandpa's interest.

"I got that picture from an antique store, isn't it cool? I wish I knew more about those guys and what they did in the war. I've even tried looking on the internet. I know they were with the 13th Air Force serving in the Pacific, they were called the Cactus Air Force."

The old man takes the picture off the wall and holds it in his hands, never looking at the boy. His focus locks on the picture.

Holden asks, "I bet you don't know what kind of plane that is."

The old man whispers as if he were recalling a deep secret. Without looking up he mumbles, "It's a Liberator, a B-24. It was in Guadalcanal, 1943." He pauses for a moment and then says:

"I know these guys; I met some of them when I was in the hospital. Three of them came to the Carney Field Hospital a few weeks after the Munda raid."

Holden says, "I found a couple of the names that were on the back of the picture, but I don't know…"

The grandfather interrupts with, "They were with the 5th Bomb Group. They had some patch on their jackets with a skull and wings." The boy grabs his tablet and reads:

"First Lieutenant, Oscar Fitzhenry-Pilot." His grandfather points to the picture of Fitz.

"Second Lieutenant, G.R.Houser-Co-Pilot", again he points to him in the picture. The boy was amazed and says,

"That's all the information I have so far."

His grandfather points to another man and says, "That guy was there too, he was the navigator. They called him Clincher."

Holden stares at his grandfather in awe of what he has just been told. He hurriedly writes down the new information.

The boy and his grandfather go outside to the patio in the backyard and sit at the table. Holden has his tablet and takes notes as his grandfather, smoking a cigar, tells him all about his experience on Munda in 1943. He tells the boy about some Army Air Corps guys, from a B-24, visiting him and some other Marines in the hospital.

"We were all working together and needed each other's help. My platoon was pinned down in a gully and in the very early morning, just as the sun was coming up, the bombing began." He reflects, "Squadrons of B-24s, B-17s and B-25s were escorted by probably a hundred fighters. Those heavy bombers came in low and it rained bombs from the sky, the sound was like thunder."

He went on to say, "The Marines had to capture that airstrip. It was the halfway point to New Ireland and the Air Corps needed it to be able to refuel."

Holden writes furiously as his grandfather recalls incidents of his service in the Pacific in 1943.

"It feels like a lifetime ago, and yet, sometimes I can remember like it was yesterday. There was so much bombing that morning that the air was thick with smoke and haze. Most of the Japanese on Munda died from the concussive force of the bombs. We took the airstrip and the Air Corps was able to advance up the Solomon Islands to the next target."

The old man pauses for a moment and looks into the face of his grandson. "Holden, I know it's something you don't quite understand just yet, but we were all young men just doing our jobs. We thought we were invincible. I suppose that's the folly of youth. We were fighting an enemy that attacked us at Pearl Harbor; we were fighting for our freedom. The war took the lives of thousands of brave young men that thought they were invincible too."

The old man takes a long puff on his cigar and gently blows out smoke. "You know son; some branches of the military are always claiming the war could not have ended with out 'their' efforts. The truth is; we all needed each other. Everyone did their part. We all had the same objective; to win this war and go home. I'm proud of my service as a Marine and I'm equally proud of the sacrifices all the other branches performed, especially the Army Air Corps.

"I think of people like then-Colonel Jimmy Doolittle, and 16 crews, flying B-25s off a carrier and bombing Tokyo in April 1942. The Air Corps and all those fly boys truly took this war to the Japanese on their soil. It was the Army Air Corps that brought this war to an end in August 1945, flying in B-29s. We were all brave young men protecting and sacrificing for our home and our futures."

The old Marine takes another long puff on his cigar, looks at his grandson and says, "You, son, are a part of that future," then smiles.

The following morning, the sun has risen and an elderly man is sitting in a comfortable chair in his family room. The room is adorned with several family photos. The television is a background diversion as he works on a crossword puzzle. His wife walks into the room and hands him a glass of orange juice saying, "You forgot to take your pills this morning." He dutifully takes the pills from her hand, swallows them and sets the glass back on the end table next to him. "Thanks babe." She leaves the room with their two Jack Russell terriers following her every move. He returns to his puzzle when he is interrupted by the phone ringing. He fumbles with the TV remote to hit the mute button, sets it down and then reaches for the phone.

"Hello?" A voice from the past answers,

"Hey Houser, wake up! We have a raid on Kahili this morning."

The old man chuckles loudly and says, "Kahili? Only if we bring Clincher with us! Fitz, how are you doing old boy?"

EPILOGUE

▼

On December 30, 1943, the crew of the Pretty Prairie Special, piloted by Colonel Marion Unruh, was last seen going down near the southern tip of New Ireland. The following day, the crew of Scootin' Thunder found the colonel and seven men from his crew, stranded on a beach waving a parachute. Scootin' Thunder and two other B-24s, circled the survivors three times. With each pass they came in lower, dropping survival supplies to the men on the beach. Captain Fitzhenry radioed the location of the downed crew and departed, not wanting to draw any further attention to the stranded soldiers. It was not learned until after the war that all eleven men bailed out of the doomed plane. Two of the crew members drowned in the crash, two starved to death and six men were executed by the Japanese. Colonel Unruh was captured by the Japanese on January 15, 1944; 16 days after his plane went down. He was taken back to Japan where he was placed in a prisoner of war camp at Rokuroshi, where he stayed for the duration of the war. His first eight months at the camp were spent in solitary confinement. The U.S. soldiers were liberated on September 8, 1945.

In a Memorial Day address in 1946 the colonel expressed his thoughts about the war to the crowd. "I think I know what was at stake. It was our freedom. A freedom that we have taken for granted and which we fail to appreciate until it is taken away. Believe me...we fought for our families, our homes and our country. Unless you have faced our late enemies and had been a victim of their vitriolic hatred, this is hard to believe. Nevertheless, we know it happened to the nations defeated by Germany and Japan. It is freedom from that which we fought. Any man that would object and not fight for the freedom which we now have, does not, in my opinion, deserve to enjoy this freedom."

The Colonel returned to his wife and two sons and retired from the service in 1959. He was killed in 1968 in an experimental plane he built in Pretty Prairie, Kansas.

Oscar Fitzhenry completed 64 combat missions and remained in the service for 20 years retiring as a lieutenant colonel and a command pilot in 1962. Oscar got his master's degree and is a real estate broker/developer. He is married with four children and 10 grandchildren and resides in South Carolina. I asked Oscar about all his combat missions and he told me: "Not to take anything away from the heroes that died relatively quickly, the real heroes got up morning after morning after morning, climbed on those planes and flew the missions. That took guts and courage."

Bill Garman went on to become the president of Occidental Chemical Company. Bill was married with two children. He retired to Palm Springs and passed away in 2000.

Bill Harris became a restaurant business owner and lives in Riverside with his wife. He still flies his own plane and spends a great deal of time as a consultant to new restaurant ventures.

Bob Houser completed 45 combat missions and after six years of service left the Air Corps as a captain. He pursued journalism and moved his family to Southern California where he retired after nearly 40 years as the political editor for the Long Beach Press-Telegram. He is married with seven children, five grandchildren and one great-grandson. Thankfully, he exhibited his journalistic skills at a young age, with the eyes and ears of a reporter, and wrote religiously in his diary.

Scootin' Thunder, the B-24D, survived the war in the Pacific, bringing all of her crews back safely from harm's way. She was flown back to Altus (Oklahoma) Airbase and was used in the training of new pilots and crews. Nearer to 1945 she was sold to the Reconstruction Finance Corporation for either Foreign Service or scrap; a sad ending to a beautiful plane that served her crew and country so well.

AFTERWORD

The crew picture of Scootin' Thunder has always sparked my imagination. My initial perspective as a small child was, "Who are all those old guys standing with dad?" The older I got my perspective changed from, "Who are all these men and what did they do in the war?" to "These guys were all so young; some of them were just boys."

My father, like many men of his generation, did not speak about his service during World War II. To him and countless others they were just doing their jobs. Initially, I wanted to inform my brothers and sisters about our dad's experiences as a co-pilot in the USAAC. After reading through his diary I constructed a spreadsheet of all his combat missions and realized there was a wonderful story unfolding that none of us had ever realized. I read about the transformation of young guys into a crew who accepted the challenges to become men. Throughout this process they formed a bond that tested them each time they got on their plane and faced another combat situation.

I soon discovered through all my additional readings on the war in the South Pacific that most stories have been written from the Marine or Navy point of view and very little from the Army Air Corps. This tribute is not just for the ten crew members of Scootin' Thunder but for all the young men of the 13th Air Force who forged bonds with their crews and faced similar threats and jeopardy. These young men displayed courage, strength and the fortitude to succeed against an aggressor, uniting them in their patriotism and seeing them through to its conclusion. All these men, including my father, Bob Houser, are heroes.

978-0-595-40337-0
0-595-40337-9

Printed in the United States
129969LV00002B/31/A